Discovering the
Old Testament

To Ron Warder and Iris Mingay
on their wedding day,
21 May 2005 AD

Discovering the Old Testament

Alec Motyer

Crossway Books Leicester

CROSSWAY BOOKS
38 De Montfort Street, Leicester LE1 7GP, England
Email: ivp@ivp-editorial.co.uk
Website: www.ivpbooks.com

First published 2006

British Library Cataloguing in Publication Data
A catalogue record for this book is available from the British Library.

ISBN–13: 978–1–85684–226–6
ISBN–10: 1–85684–226–6

Set in Palatino
Typeset in Great Britain by Avocet Typeset, Chilton, Aylesbury, Bucks
Printed and bound in Great Britain by Bookmarque Ltd, Croydon, Surrey

CONTENTS

Preface 7
About this voyage of discovery 8

Part one: Is there such a thing as the Old Testament?

1 Answer: No ... yes ... It all depends! 15
2 Thinking straight about salvation and law 25
3 The Jesus book 33
4 So what's in it for me? I'm New Testament! 38

Part two: Come for a walk through the Old Testament

5 No-hopers and their persistent God:
Genesis 12 – Deuteronomy 34 51
6 The whole world not forgotten: Genesis 1 – 11 61
7 'He's the image of his Father!' 68
8 At home with the holy God 77
9 Great stories, one story 89
10 What hymn book do you use? 105
11 A skeleton in the cupboard 116
12 Five self-portraits 129
13 Who and when, but above all, why and what 142
14 All this – and wisdom too! 155

Part three: Looking back, looking on, looking up

15 So what is the Old Testament saying to us? 175
16 What a hope! 190

Books for further reading 205

Preface

Dr David McKay very kindly invited me, a few years ago, to write articles on the Old Testament for the magazine of the Reformed Presbyterian Church in Northern Ireland. The series was called 'Meet the Old Testament', but the articles have been pushed around, adapted, extended, altered, added to, subtracted from, and rewritten to such an extent that Dr McKay will hardly recognize the result, and this book is very different from that series ...

Inevitably, though, those who knew me when I taught Old Testament and Hebrew at Clifton Theological College, Tyndale Hall and Trinity College, Bristol, or who have read my other books, or attended conferences where I spoke, may possibly have their memories jogged, for most of this material has done the rounds one way or another.

One of God's greatest blessings to me is that, from infancy, I was told the Bible stories. They belong with my earliest memories, and I cannot recall a time when I did not love the Bible and revere it as the Word of God. It is against this background that I have written this book. A great many passing years and a reasonable amount of reading and study have served to deepen and sharpen those early convictions. The book we call the Holy Bible – both the longer, first part (the Old Testament) and the shorter, second part (the New Testament) – is God's Word written. Those who believe in our Lord Jesus Christ have no deeper need, nor indeed a more fruitful enrichment, than to understand, love and obey what he has revealed.

I pray that God will allow *Discovering the Old Testament* to play some small part towards that end.

Alec Motyer

About this voyage of discovery: a personal travelogue and plea

You may be one of the world's natural travellers, able to set off on a journey with a happy heart and an undistracted mind, but if (like me) you are a natural 'stay-at-home', you will know what it is to groan in spirit and ask, 'Do I have to?'

Maybe, therefore, you are already asking what is the point of attempting a journey through the thirty-nine books, thirty-one (or more) writers, and at least two thousand years of the Old Testament. You are contented in Christ, busy in your church, and find the New Testament more than enough to be going on with. So 'Why bother with the Old?' you may well be asking, with the implied heartfelt plea, 'Leave me alone!'

Jesus is the answer

Fortunately, the 'Why bother?' question is easily answered. What we call 'the Old Testament' was the Bible that Jesus revered, treasured, lived by and called 'the Word of God'. That happy thought should be enough to dispel our groans and even make us avid for the journey. It is our highest honour and our best ambition to 'resemble the Son of God' (cf. Hebrews 7:3). Long years ago we used to sing a song with the chorus-line, 'Like Jesus, like Jesus, I want to be like Jesus', but so often we frittered away our (fitful) ambition for Christlikeness by focusing on idealistic targets – like matching his holiness! The aim of this 'voyage of discovery' is to earth our ambition in an achievable goal: he knew, loved and obeyed the Word of God – the 'Old' Testament. So then, let us set out on our journey resolved to be like him!

The supreme 'Bible Man'

In his recorded words, the Lord Jesus Christ quoted directly from at least twenty-one books of the Old Testament. He handled the Scriptures with ease and fluency. He crushed the temptations of Satan with prompt and apt words from Deuteronomy. In a word, he knew thoroughly books which we might have difficulty even in finding! But there is more. In the Garden of Gethsemane (Matthew 26:51–54) the impulsively brave Peter was ready to make a fight of it, but Jesus refused to go the way of this very 'just war'. In his view, it was not only that those who take the sword die by it, but fundamentally, that he – who needed no man's sword, he who had at his beck and call legions of angels – rather, was determined that in his life 'the Scriptures' must 'be fulfilled'. He really was the supreme 'Bible Man'. Indeed, John tells us that, on the cross, it was not the raging dehydration of a crucified victim that made him say, 'I am thirsty.' It was that the Scripture might be fulfilled (John 19:28). Would we be mistaken to think that, as he hung there, Jesus was searching, in his capacious memory, through the length and breadth of Scripture, to make sure he had in fact done all that the Father desired, and, so as to leave no stone unturned, that he determined to cover also this one item in Psalm 22?

In any case, that is how he valued the Old Testament Scripture, and should we not do the same?

Enjoy – and make the effort

The old-time gold-rush prospectors used to say, 'There's gold in them there hills!' I can promise you that, as together we look out over the craggy peaks of the Old Testament and delve into its deep ravines, not only gold, but also diamonds and treasures in abundance are waiting to be mined.

▶ Fourteen out of the thirty-nine books of the Old Testament are devoted to the most gripping stories you will ever read, and the most carefully drawn character studies – from the gormless buffoon Samson, who could never resist either a joke or a girl, to the gentle Isaac, who never seemed to do anything; from the stumbling but believing Abraham to the politician turned builder, Nehemiah; and, among the kings, the rosy-cheeked David who found it hard to grow up, the nincompoop Rehoboam who lost his inheritance, the good-hearted but inept Hezekiah who was given a job 'above his ceiling', and the unbelievably stupid Zedekiah who lost it all. Don't, in the first instance, fuss over 'getting a message' or 'finding a blessed thought' in the stories. Just enjoy them – even at the level of 'ripping yarns'. Soon they will begin to speak back to you.

▶ Get to grips with the way Hebrew poetry 'works' – for, simply on the level of literature, you won't find higher or more satisfying poets than in the Psalms. Greek and Latin classical verse developed a highly complex form governed by detailed and intricate rules. The poet revealed his skill by the beauty and sensitivity with which he presented his material within that demanding form. Hebrew poetry is quite different. Meaning – the presentation of the truth – dominates all, and form is flexibly subservient to message. Rhythm is reckoned not by stressed and unstressed syllables but by significant (meaningful) words – perhaps three main words in one line and two in the next, or three in each. This is often traceable even in translation, and as we read we can note how everything is subordinated to what the poet wants to say.

In addition, Hebrew poets used the literary feature known as parallelism – saying broadly the same thing twice. Yet this is never mere repetition; the parallel line adds something fresh: it also serves the cause of the truth by building up the fuller presentation. Again, don't start by looking for a 'message'. Try to catch the rhythm and beat of the 'significant words' and the balancing of one statement with another. Read the poetry as poetry.

► But, of course, there is more to the Old Testament than good stories to be enjoyed and high poetry to be savoured. The Lord is the 'hero' of his own book, and the 'point' of the book is to reveal him. This is, pre-eminently, the work of the prophets. As the preachers, teachers and headline-makers of their day, their task was to 'forth-tell' the truth about the Lord. They were not, as a matter of fact, innovators, but exponents of the foundational truth laid down by Moses. Part of their 'forth-telling' was, of course, 'fore-telling' what the Lord was about to do. But don't come to them in order to draw up a calendar. Ask (as we shall see) every passage the same questions: 'What?' – what is the prophet saying here? – and 'Why?' – why is he saying it? Because what the prophet said then is what he is saying now; the old message is the answer to the new questions.

Know your enemy

All this amounts to a call to get reading and keep reading. The Old Testament is a strange country to us mainly because we don't walk up and down in it enough – and often enough. Ignorance is the enemy, and there's only one way to beat it!

I hope that reading through this book will prove to be the voyage of discovery you need. But remember, there are no short cuts. Take your time. Please look up the cross-references – and when you come to the daily reading section at the end of each chapter – well, please don't skimp on your homework!

The Lord knew what he was doing when he edited his book into its final form, and the large bit which comes first, which we call 'the Old Testament', is not 'old' at all. It is where the Lord intends us to start, and through it he intends to introduce himself to us.

PART ONE

Is there such a thing as the Old Testament?

Answer: No ... yes ... It all depends!

Ask a silly question and get a silly answer! But is it really so silly to ask if there is such a thing as the Old Testament?

Ask Peter

When Peter was preaching on the day of the Pentecost, he quoted from Joel (2:28–32; Acts 2:17ff.) and from the Psalms (16:8–11; Acts 2:25; Psalm 110:1; Acts 2:34). But suppose someone had asked him afterwards, 'Why do you quote from the Old Testament?' He probably would not have understood. 'Quote from the what?' he might have asked.

And he did not change as the years passed. Looking back on his life, when he sensed his death was near, he wanted more than anything else to prepare the church for the future. Among other things, he warned about people who twist the meaning of Paul's epistles – just as, he says, they also do to 'the other Scriptures' (2 Peter 3:15–16). He does not say, as we might have done, 'the Scriptures of the New Testament, just as they do to those of the Old'. Rather, it comes naturally to him to link together the inspired writings of the apostles and the inherited, in-spired writings of prophets and others, seeing them as a single item called 'the Scriptures'.

Paul, too

Paul had the same idea. When he came to the end of his

earthly career, he too sensed that a line was about to be drawn across church history, marking off what went before, the 'apostolic' years, from what would follow, the 'post-apostolic' years. So he wrote to Timothy to prepare him and the church for what lay ahead, when 'the apostles' would be a thing of the past.

The apostles had provided a visible centre and focal point for the church, and were the earthly revealers of God's truth. What would be the focal point (if any) round which the church would gather when they were no longer available? What hallmark would distinguish the true church from false claimants, those alternative groups (2 Timothy 4:3–4) which Paul foresaw arising?

The hallmark

In each of the four chapters of 2 Timothy, Paul offers the same answer. It is this:

▶ 'What you heard from me, keep as the pattern of sound teaching ...' (1:13)

▶ 'as one ... who correctly handles the word of truth' (2:15)

▶ 'Preach the Word' (4:2).

And if we ask, what is this 'pattern', this 'word of truth'? Chapter 3 replies like this: first, Paul points to his own teaching, handed on to Timothy: 'You know all about my teaching ... continue in what you have learned' (3:10, 14). Secondly, there is what he calls (literally translated) the 'sacred writings' – what we call 'the Old Testament' – which Timothy has learned from babyhood (3:15). Then, combining these two together, Paul goes straight to the point: 'All Scripture is God-breathed and useful...' (3:16).

Not 'two testaments', just 'one Bible' ... So?

Once more, then, where we would, so to speak, 'see double'

in terms of the Old and the New Testaments, it was natural for the apostles to 'see straight' and speak of a single item called 'the Scriptures'.

How right are we, then, to talk about an 'Old' Testament? To be sure, we can hardly avoid doing so. Long-standing habit, not to mention the continuing efforts of Bible printers, with their sad blank page separating Malachi from Matthew, guarantee that it is not open to us to undo now what usage has so firmly established. We just have to go on calling the first and larger bit of our Bibles 'the Old Testament', but it is really important that we should try to understand why Peter and Paul did not see things that way. In many respects, it is easy to explain why we have divided into two what they saw as one, but it is absolutely vital to understand why they saw as one what we have divided into two!

A promise made, a promise kept

Try asking Peter again: 'So why do you keep quoting the Old Testament?' He might well reply: 'Old Testament? That's not what it *is*; that's what it's *about*.'

Within the Bible, a 'testament' is not a book, it's a promise – actually a covenant promise from God. That is, a promise pledged, guaranteed, made to us by God of his own free will and choice, a promise he has bound himself to keep.

Start with Noah

The actual word 'covenant' is first used (Genesis 6:18) in connection with Noah and the flood, and it came about like this. In spite of belonging to a whole world that was under God's judgment (6:5–7), *Noah found grace* (6:8). This is a very exact translation but it really *means* that grace found Noah. For, as Genesis 6:5–7 makes plain, the whole human race (including Noah, of course) was caught up in sin (verse 5), was a grief to God (verse 6), and was under his judgment of death (verse 7). What made Noah different was not his distinctive life (verse 9) – that was some-thing which followed from the grace he was given (verse 8). Yes, grace made him different and distinctive among his contemporaries, but grace itself can never be merited. It is God's free, undeserved favour.

In his grace the Lord saved Noah when judgment fell on the rest of the world through the great flood, and it is this work of salvation which is the centrepiece of God's covenant promise. Notice how Genesis makes a contrast: 'I am going to bring floodwaters … to destroy all life … Everything on earth will perish. But I will establish [literally implement] my covenant with you, and you will enter the ark' (Genesis 6:17–18). Noah is contrasted with all others as the individual marked out for salvation; the means of that salvation is the ark; and the ground of his salvation is the covenant-promise of God.

This is what 'covenant' means all through the Bible: God's covenant is his pledged determination to save those whom he has chosen.

Next, Abraham

In turn, Abraham became the heir of this covenant. He had two pressing needs, and the Lord now made his covenant promise in such a way that these needs were covered by it. First, Abram (as he was then, Genesis 15) was childless. It seems that, in accord with one of the legal customs of the day, he had 'adopted' his chief servant, Eliezer (15:2–3), to inherit (and to look after the funeral arrangements). But he had no son of his very own. Secondly, Abram was a wanderer, without fixed address – no son to call his own and no place to call his own! But the Lord had covenant promises to make, pledging both descendants and a homeland (15:4–5, 18–21),

But things did not stop there. When the Lord spelled out his promise in a fuller way, he even went beyond these two things. Genesis 17:4–8 records the fullest form of the Lord's promise to Abram. It came in four parts:

1. Personal: A transformation (verse 5)

'Abram' became 'Abraham'. In Hebrew, 'Abram' sounds like 'Exalted Father', and 'Abraham' like 'Father of a Crowd'. The man who had no children will have them in abundance. Abraham is now the new man, transformed by divine promise and power, with new abilities and prospects.

2. National: A royal nation (verse 6)

The Lord had promised 'fruitfulness' (Genesis 15:5), expressed here in a family of 'nations' and their 'kings'. We can only wonder what Abraham made of all this at the time. We have the benefit of hindsight. We know how Abraham's grandson Jacob had twelve sons (Genesis 29 – 30), how they became the twelve-tribe nation of 'Israel' (Exodus 1:1), how the 'Israel' of the Old Testament is the 'Israel of God' of Galatians 6:16, the innumerable company (Revelation 7:9) of those who belong to Jesus, and how Jesus is also the son of David, possessor of the throne and reigning for ever (Luke 1:32–33). The Lord's promises are like that: he never fails to keep them, but he keeps them in a way that outshines anything that could have been foreseen at the start.

3. Spiritual: A relationship

There is a 'family' principle in the Lord's covenant-making. His promises include our children. Over and over he said to Noah, 'you and your sons' (e.g. Genesis 6:18; 7:1). At Passover the whole family was brought under the sheltering blood of the slain lamb (Exodus 12:21–27), and the same family principle was repeated by Peter when he said, 'the promise is for you and your children' (Acts 2:39). So to Abraham, God said, 'your God and the God of your descendants after you' (Genesis 17:7). Notice that these words express his commitment, the undertaking he makes, sovereignly and unilaterally, in his covenant promise. The promise embraces the children of believers.

4. Territorial: A land to live in

Genesis 17:8 confirms the promise covenanted in 15:18–20. Even in the halcyon days of David and Solomon (e.g. 1 Kings 4:21, 24), Israel never actually possessed all the land mentioned here. After Solomon the kingdom split into two tiny kingdoms (1 Kings 12) along the Jordan in Palestine. In 722 BC the northern kingdom, Israel, was terminated by the Assyrian superpower. From the time of Ahaz (c. 735 BC, 2 Kings 16:7) even the monarchy of David became a puppet state, and never again did a free, sovereign king sit on David's throne until the One came whose right it is to reign (Luke 1:32–33), and, as Jesus taught, the territorial promises of the Old Testament reached their intended fulfilment in the kingdom 'not of this world' (John 18:36) and the heavenly Jerusalem (Hebrews 12:22; Revelation 21).

History is his story

One of the reasons why so much of the Old Testament is concerned with history is to teach us that God really does stand by his promises, through thick and thin, including when they are tested out by the buffetings of life. Thus, when Abraham's descendants were gripped by Egyptian slavery (Exodus 1:11–14), the promise of a land of their own must have seemed, to human eyes, to have worn a bit threadbare. And when they were under threat of genocide (Exodus 1:22), did it seem as if God had really meant it, when he had pledged himself to be their God? But had God really forgotten either them or his promises? The marvellous story of the Exodus is deliberately told in the only terms which suit its reality: the Lord remembered his covenant (Exodus 2:24) and brought his people out of bondage and into actual ownership of the promised land (Joshua 21:45; 23:14).

Untiring faithfulness

Yet as the story unfolds, it is clear that all is by no means well. While the book of Judges only covers a single period of the history of the people of God, in one sense it tells the whole story. They are in the land, yet their tenure is constantly imperilled. There are enemies on every side, often within the confines of the land itself, not infrequently lording it over God's heritage. The cause of all this, however, is in the people themselves. Judges 2:11–23 speaks for all the history books of the Old Testament: faithlessness, disobedience and apostasy bring upon the covenant people the punishments of their holy God – actions elsewhere called 'the curses' (Deuteronomy 29:21) and the 'vengeance of the covenant' (Leviticus 26:25).

Yet, out of all this experience of failure to enter into the fullness of what God had promised – as the Bible would say, to inherit the promises (e.g. Hebrews 6:12) – arose the longing that somehow this situation might be remedied, and, along with the longing, the certainty that the Lord would stand by his word, and that ... some day ...!

Jeremiah and the new covenant

It fell to Jeremiah to be the first to use the words 'new covenant', and to say what they would mean (Jeremiah 31:31–34).

▶ First, he exposed where the fault lay: 'they broke my covenant, although I was a husband to them' (verse 32). He used marriage to illustrate the Lord's covenant relationship with them. On the one hand, the Lord had fully discharged all his obligations as the divine 'Husband'. But the relationship was too exacting for human frailty and 'they broke' it.

▶ Secondly, Jeremiah foretold how this situation will be remedied. The Lord will not relax his standards out of consideration for human weakness and failure, or change his ways of working. His 'law' remains the same. The word here (as so often) has a broad meaning and a more specific meaning. In its broad sense it means all that the Lord has revealed to his people, for the word 'law' (*torah*) actually means 'teaching' – all that the Lord has taught them about himself, his ways, his dealings with his people, his plan for their lives, his rules and commandments. It is still all 'my law' and 'carries over' into the new covenant. But Jeremiah will have had in mind also the specific sense of 'the law of Moses' (cf. Deuteronomy 4:2, 5, 13–14). On its moral side, this law was summarized in the Ten Commandments (Exodus 20:2–17; Deuteronomy 5:5–21), and on its religious side, it covered all the regulations regarding the sacrifices by which atonement was made and sin forgiven (cf. Leviticus 1:4; 4:27–31). This too is an abiding revelation of the Lord, part of his revealed 'teaching', and will have its place in the new Covenant. In Jeremiah's understanding, then, so much remains the same, but with one great change: the Lord promised through him to create for his people a new inner constitution, a 'heart' shaped to match all that was in his law, and designed for obedience (and enjoyment). This is the truth expressed so vividly as writing the law on the heart.

▶ Thirdly (verse 34), how will all this be accomplished? The Lord will somehow finally deal with his people's sins – so fully and finally that even he will retain no spark of memory of them. Jeremiah does not say how this will happen, but in the light of the two divisions of the law of Moses noted above (the moral and the religious, the rules to obey and the way of atonement for disobedience), it is not hard to guess the answer: the Lord's provisions for atonement (cf. Leviticus 17:11) will be replicated in some great and all-sufficient sacrifice, foreshadowed on the day of atonement (Leviticus 16:21–22) and fulfilled in Jesus (Hebrews 10:1–18).

If anything could ever compel us to stop seeing our Bibles in two parts, and to begin thinking instead of one

Scripture, it would be the realization that 'new' testament is an 'old' testament idea, which, far from dividing the Bible into two, demands that we recognize it as a single whole. Hebrews 10:10–18 could not be more explicit. Here is the will of the Father purposing a final offering for sin (verse 10); here is the work of the Son, offering 'one sacrifice for sins for ever' (verses 11–14); and here is the witness of the Holy Spirit, who takes up the very words he had once spoken through Jeremiah 600 years previously in order to affirm that in Christ the final dealing with sin has been accomplished (verses 15–18).

A thought a day for seven days

Whatever you do, you must not let these verses replace or interrupt your existing plan of daily Bible reading. Think of this as Bible reading for elevenses – something to do along with your morning coffee. Just fit it in somewhere as an extra, a way of thinking further about the theme of the last chapter while launching into the next.

You will, of course, have looked up all the references given in Chapter 1, but here are a few of them to chew over again. They are really important:

Day 1
Noah and the covenant: Genesis 6:8, 17–18. God's covenant is a work of grace providing protection from his just judgment.

Day 2
Abraham and the covenant: Genesis 17:1, 3–8. God's covenant is full of promises and expects a distinct life.

Day 3
Noah and Abraham are models for us today: Hebrews 11:7–10. They lived and persevered under the Word of God.

Day 4
Jeremiah and the new covenant: Jeremiah 31:31–34. The old law, the new people, the final dealing with sin.

Day 5
Paul describes the Bible: 2 Timothy 3:10–17. It 'grew' in two stages (verses 10, 15, 'the holy writings') It is all one (verse 16, 'Scripture'), originating in God ('God-breathed').

Day 6
Peter describes the Bible and its writers: 2 Peter 1:20–21. 'Prophecy' from God, about God. Special men, specially inspired, received the word which came from God.

Day 7
Jesus and the Bible: Matthew 26:52–54; Luke 24:27. He is the Bible's subject and servant.

Questions

1. Do you view the Bible in two distinct parts? What difference does it make to consider it as one whole message from God?
2. What foretastes of Jesus' work do you discern in the stories of the Old Testament characters? Are there any surprises for you?
3. As Christians living after both the Old and New Testaments what is God's covenant with us today? How does it (like Abraham) affect us personally, affect our nation, affect our family and affect the land?

Thinking straight about salvation and law

God's covenant, however, is only one of many factors which make the Bible a single book. Within the covenant there lie other great unifying themes. Take, first, the way of salvation.

We must ask Noah, Abraham and Old Testament Israel how they actually entered into the experience of salvation and imagine how they would reply. The answer is clear from the stories.

Noah

The word of God came to Noah and he believed (Genesis 6:11–22), and acted upon it – a marvellous example of sheer faith in the word of God. Think of the colossal size of the ark, the enormous amount of material and work to make it, and probably the mockery from the onlookers that Noah had to endure. And why did Noah build the ark? Just because God said so! That's faith: action taken on the basis of the word of God – not a 'leap in the dark' but a leap into the light of God's revealed truth.

Abraham

In the same way, the word of God came to Abram (as he then was), and he believed it. It was initially a word directly related to his felt needs: you shall have descendants more numerous than can be counted (Genesis 15:5). Abram entered into the reality of this promise by choosing to believe what God said, rather than believing the evidence of his own childlessness, for which, humanly speaking, there was no remedy (cf. Romans 4:16–22; Hebrews 11:17–19). Subsequently, when God came to him with the even more far-reaching promise that he, the Lord, of his own volition, had committed himself to be the God of Abraham and of his descendants for ever, Abraham again responded obediently (Genesis 17:1–14, 23). And just as on an earlier occasion (Genesis 9:11–17) God had confirmed his promise to Noah by means of the sign of the rainbow, so God gave to Abraham the sign of circumcision, to mark off from all others the man to whom the covenant promises had been made. By his obedience in imposing this sign on himself and his household, Abraham declared his faith in the promises which the sign bestowed and confirmed.

Israel

When we move on to the situation of Israel in Egypt, the truth is the same. If we had been in a position to question those whom the Lord redeemed (Exodus 6:6), asking how they had entered into this blessing, someone could well have replied: 'I was a slave, under sentence of death, helpless and with no hope. A man named Moses said that, if we killed a lamb and sprinkled its blood round our doors and then sheltered under the blood, we would be safe when the Lord came in judgment into Egypt, and we would come out, redeemed, and liberated. I believed what the Lord promised. I and my family sheltered under the blood of the lamb, and we were indeed redeemed.' As we shall see in greater detail presently, the story told in Exodus 12 cannot be explained by any other interpretation than this: the people entered into the proffered salvation by believing the promises of God.

New and old, hand in glove, heads and tails

All this is just what we read in the New Testament regarding the way of salvation. The blood by which the covenant is inaugurated (Exodus 24:8) is now the blood of Jesus (Luke 22:20). He is the 'Lamb of God' (John 1:29, 35), and, as John 1:12 puts it with beautiful clarity, we become the children of God by 'receiving' and 'believing in' Jesus. The promises of God are summed up, concentrated and fulfilled in Jesus (2 Corinthians 1:20), and salvation is, as always throughout the Bible from beginning to end, by faith.

In spite of all this, however, crowds of people live with a delusion. They think that the Old Testament teaches salvation by works, while it is only in the New Testament that the lesson is learned that this is a vain hope, and salvation by works is replaced by salvation through grace alone, by faith alone.

Beware of the Pharisees – read the Psalms

We are, of course, helped to make this common but false contrast between the Testaments by assuming that the Pharisees (whom we meet in the Gospels as opponents of Jesus) were typical representatives and products of the Old Testament. This could not be more misleading. Remember that Jesus described them as a 'plant which my heavenly Father has not planted' (Matthew 15:13) – that is, an apostate (or deserting) body. Indeed, Jesus is saying, far from being representatives of the Old Testament, they are, from its point of view, a heresy. Their agonized bondage to rules and regulations, and the carping, unhappy spirit these appear to have generated, would, on the contrary, be a poor advertisement for the Old Testament.

When we read the Psalms, it is like looking through a huge picture window into the heart of the old covenant church. Think of the exuberance of the religious life we find there – the calls to sing, to shout aloud, to clap and make music (Psalms 95:1; 47:1; 150:3–5). Think of the depth of personal devotion shown (18:1–2), and the reverence for the Lord's name (44:20). Above all, listen to the voice that calls out with delight, 'Oh, how I love your law!' (119:97). Imagine it: God's law something to love! All those commandments are a delight!

Clearly, we had better try to start all over again and think straight about God's law. What is it? Why did God give it? And what is its place in the Bible's scheme of things? Big questions, and actually every bit as important as they are big.

Adam

The Lord's people have always been marked out by their possession of the Lord's word. He has never left us ignorant about himself and what he desires for us.

It started with Adam. In the Garden, God's sole requirement of him was that he should obey what the Lord said. The whole bounty of God's Garden was there for Adam to enjoy (Genesis 2:16), but always on condition of obeying one single law, the law concerning the tree of the knowledge of good and evil (2:17). Adam could revel in all the richness and lavishness of the goodness of God as long as he obeyed the word of God. He did not work his way into the Garden by obedience. The Garden was planted and he was put in it by divine decision and action (2:8, 15). But, once there, enjoyment of the Garden's bounty was conditional on obeying the single law, the word of God.

We need to see, then, that grace and law, law and grace belong together. In Genesis 2, God's grace is his sheer lavishness, given freely by God's will and choice to Adam, not earned but given. Its enjoyment, however, required obedience to the whole law of God, the single and simple precept of the tree of knowledge. Obey and enjoy or disobey and forfeit. Law and grace are not enemies. They do not oppose or fight each other. By grace Adam and his wife are in the Garden, with its lavishness all around them – and God 'richly provides us with everything for our enjoyment' (1 Timothy 6:17). By keeping God's law we are free to enjoy too. His law is a way of life (Leviticus 18:5; Acts 5:32).

Noah and Abraham

It was the same for Noah (whom we met earlier). His story begins with the statement that he *found grace* (Genesis 6:8). This (literal and accurate) wording might suggest that he was looking for it, but the formula '*x* found grace' always implies no worthiness or deserving on the part of the recipient, but the free gift of some benefit (e.g. Ruth 2:10). The reality behind the wording is that 'grace found Noah'. But as soon as grace touched Noah's life, a transformation took place (Genesis 6:9), and this was worked out as a life of obedience to God in building (6:22) and peopling (7:5) the ark, entering (7:1) and leaving it (8:15), only by God's command. 'Noah did everything just as God commanded him' (6:22; 7:5). When we recall the extraordinary thing he did – building the ark – we see another side to it: Noah not only did *what* the Lord commanded, but he did it *because* the Lord commanded it. This was sheer obedience. Only the Lord could decide to favour Noah with his grace (6:8), and to protect him with his covenant (6:18). But once within the circle of grace, and within the promises of the covenant, Noah enjoyed their benefits by obeying what the Lord commanded, and so came safely through the flood.

The same is true of Abraham. Everything began in the mind and purpose of God. It was the Lord who called him (Genesis 12:1), promised him future fruitfulness and greatness (12:2), and put him at the centre of his plan to bless the world (12:3). It was the Lord who brought him out from Ur, and promised him a new land (15:7) with innumerable descendants (15:4) and future victories (15:18–21), all without any cooperative action (never mind deserving action) on Abram's part. It was the Lord who freely made the detailed promises of 17:1–8. As the Bible would teach us to put it, it was 'all of grace'. But the man to whom grace came in such abundance was called to a life of moral perfection in fellowship with God (17:1), a life of immediate (17:9) and costly (22:1–2) obedience to divine demands, of 'holding nothing back' (22:16).

Moses and Israel

We see, then, a pattern emerging: everything starts with divine grace, freely given, leading into a life of obedience to the revealed will (the law) of God. What Moses did completed the picture. We need not dwell on details at this point but we can 'cut to the chase'. The Lord 'remembered his covenant' (Exodus 2:24), and took action to deliver and redeem his helpless, enslaved people (6:6). Deliverance meant coming out of Egypt and into the Promised Land (6:8). Redemption meant being brought to the Lord (6:7). When they left Egypt, therefore, their expected target was Canaan, but, at the crucial moment (13:17; 15:22), the pillar (13:21–22) led them away from the Promised Land into the wilderness, and so to Sinai (19:1–2).

Now use all that as a visual aid

Redemption came first – and the grousing, unwilling attitude of the people (e.g. Exodus 5:20–21; 16:2; 17:2) reveals the extent to which their redemption was all of divine grace and in no way linked with merit on their part. But those whom the Lord had redeemed by his grace were brought, as a primary destination, to the mountain where they would hear the Lord's law and commit themselves to obey it (19:8; 20:1–17; 24:7).

Grace first, law second; redemption first, obedience second. The Lord's law is not a ladder by which we try to climb into God's good books; it is a way of life which he commands to those who are already, by his grace, in his good books.

James and Paul

This is precisely what the New Testament says. Faith proves itself by the life of obedience which follows from it. James, in his letter, underlines this with such gusto (e.g. 2:14–26) that he has even been accused of contradicting what Paul says about justification by faith alone, but actually their teaching is identical. When Paul calls us to 'offer [y]our bodies as living sacrifices' (Romans 12:1–3), the call is based on two facts: the first is that this is the only thoughtful, logical response to the divine mercies (verse 1); the second is that such a response is the only sufficient preparation for a life of obedience (verse 3). In other words, mercy comes first, response and obedience follow.

Everywhere Scripture gives identical teaching on this point: God's promises come to us by his grace alone. The only and sufficient response to these promises is to believe them. The only and sufficient evidence of saving faith is obedient living. Nowhere is law the way of access to grace. Everywhere obedience to law is the proof that our life has been touched and changed by grace.

Have a happy Psalms week!

The Psalms are a God-given window into the Old Testament – a window into what it teaches, for example, but chiefly into the minds and feelings of our brothers and sisters in God's covenant. If we don't end this week by desiring to be like them, we have not really entered into the Psalms.

Day 1
Holiness, without which no-one will see God: Psalm 15.

Day 2
Knowing and loving God; the power of prayer: Psalm 18:1–6.

Day 3
God's power and awesomeness: Psalms 18:7–15; 29.

Day 4
God's pardoning mercy: Psalms 51:1–7; 130.

Day 5
God the Creator: Psalm 104.

Day 6
God's Word; obeying God: Psalm 119:33–40, 97–104.

Day 7
The praise due to God's name: Psalms 145; 150.

Questions

1. Grace and mercy first. Obedience follows. As you reflect on this truth ask yourself:
   a) Whether there is an area of your life where you may be trying to earn God's favour and deserve his grace.
   b) Is there an issue upon which God is currently asking for your obedience?
   Respond to God's prompting to receive his grace and follow him in obedience.
2. How can you help Christians in your small group or church appreciate both the riches of God's grace and the clear call to obedience.

The Jesus book

We have seen enough now to allow us to describe the Bible by the words, 'progressive revelation'. When we drew lessons from the stories of Adam, Noah, Abraham and Israel, we did not have to issue a warning that those early stories might contain errors which the Bible would subsequently repudiate. We saw, on the contrary, that truth is built on truth: the earlier truth is illuminated, enlarged and completed by gradual unfoldings and revelations. The 'Old' and 'New' Testaments together form the one, progressive, cumulative volume of 'the Holy Scriptures'.

But the main reason why we must concern ourselves with the Old Testament is neither *apostolic* (that the apostles did so), nor *practical* (that without the Old, the New is unexplained). It is *dominical* – that is, the Lord Jesus requires us to do so, and, if we do not give ourselves to understanding the Old Testament, we are not following him, will not understand him, and indeed, we are displeasing and disobeying him.

Jesus and the Bible

A time-honoured way of expressing this is to say that the Old Testament is Jesus predicted, the Gospels are Jesus arrived, Acts is Jesus preached, the Epistles are Jesus explained, and Revelation is Jesus coming again. This is broadly true, and it's a delightful way of holding the whole Bible together.

The attitude of Jesus to his Bible, our Old Testament, is, first, *affirmation*: 'Until heaven and earth disappear, not the smallest letter, not the least stroke of a pen will by any means disappear from the law, till everything is accomplished' (Matthew 5:18). The smallest Hebrew letter, *yôd*, is indeed tiny, hardly more than what we would call an 'inverted comma'; the 'least stroke of a pen' is often the miniscule but important addition (like crossing a 't') whereby one letter is made different from another. The Old Testament in its written form was prized and affirmed by Jesus even to this extent.

Next, we find that the Lord Jesus *recognized* the authority of the Old Testament over the details of daily life. When he was confronted by the Pharisees on the issue of Sabbath observance, his characteristic reply was, 'Have you not read? … But if you had known what this means …' (Matthew 12:3, 5, 7). The Pharisees based their Sabbath practice narrowly on the Fourth Commandment. But Jesus insists that the totality of the Scripture must be honoured. So he found in the life of David an *example* to follow (Matthew 12:3; 1 Samuel 21:1–6), in the regulations for the priestly life an important *precept* (Matthew 12:5; Numbers 28:9–10), and in the teaching of Hosea a *principle* to be applied (Matthew 12:7; Hosea 6:6).

Thirdly, it was on this basis that Jesus lived his own life. He *submitted* to the Old Testament. So, for example, when he was confronted in Gethsemane by his enemies, and Peter would have made a brave fight of it, Jesus forbade him, saying: 'Do you think I cannot call on my Father, and he will at once put at my disposal more than twelve legions of angels?' (Matthew 26:53). In other words, it was open to Jesus on earth to live in terms of a 'hotline' to heaven which his position as the Son of God gave him; but, he added, 'how then would the Scriptures be fulfilled …?' (verse 54). He chose, above everything, to bind himself within the bounds of the Bible, the Old Testament Scriptures.

Finally, these Scriptures which Jesus affirmed, recognized and obeyed, were also *imposed* on the church. Luke chooses this as his picture of the risen Lord Jesus Christ. He records that, in the late afternoon of what we call the first Easter Day, two people (a man and his wife?) were walking home to Emmaus. As they walked, they were sharing their bewilderment about Jesus, and Jesus himself came alongside and walked with them (Luke 24:13–15). What would have been easier than immediately to open their eyes, and to solve their problem by allowing them to see him as the risen Lord? But, on the contrary, 'they were kept from recognizing him' (verse 16). For the purpose of the Risen One was to show that, just as he had refused to live in terms of direct communication with the Father, choosing rather to live in the light of the Father's will in the Bible, so he would have his church on earth live. They cannot have their problems solved by direct visions and revelations; he will not permit it. Their eyes were 'controlled' while he took the book of God, and 'beginning with Moses and all the Prophets, he explained to them what was said in all the Scriptures concerning himself' (verse 27). It was in this way that the foolish and slow heart of verse 25 became the burning heart of verse 32. It was only when the Scriptures had been explored and understood that he was ready to show himself to them in his risen glory (verse 31).

But the story does not end there. Presently the same risen Lord stood with the church in the upper room (Luke 24:36). He first declared that whatever the Scriptures foretold of him had to be fulfilled (verse 44). He then 'opened their minds so they could understand the Scriptures' (verse 45), for only thus would they grasp the message of repentance and remission which they were required to preach (verses 46–47).

This, then, is the way the risen Lord Jesus Christ looks at us today. The church on earth cannot know him and cannot preach him except as the Old Testament Scriptures teach us to understand him and to grasp his message.

What we call 'the Old Testament', Jesus called 'the word of God' (Mark 7:13); what he spoke of as something 'Moses said' (Mark 7:10) he also understood as something 'God said' (Matthew 15:4); even what began as a passing comment, unattributed to any speaker (Genesis 2:24), Jesus heard as spoken by the voice of God himself (Matthew 19:4–5).

Our task, aim and privilege is to become 'like the Son of God' in everything (cf. Hebrews 7:3), including his attitude to our Old Testament, his Bible.

A thought a day for seven days about Jesus and the Bible

By raising Jesus from the dead, God in heaven put the seal of his approval on the life Jesus lived, the works he performed, the claim he made that his saving work was 'finished', and on what he taught. So what did Jesus think about the Bible, and how did he use it?

Day 1
The Bible is permanent: Matthew 5:17–18; John 10:35.

Day 2
What the Bible says is what will happen: Luke 22:37.

Day 3
What the Bible says, God says: Matthew 19:4–5.

Day 4
Jesus' overriding concern was to obey God's Word: Matthew 26:52–54; cf. John 8:29.

Day 5
Only through the Bible can we know and share Jesus: Luke 24:25–27, 32, 45–48.

Day 6
The way to solve problems and avoid errors is to discover what the Bible says: Luke 10:26; Matthew 22:29.

Day 7
Hearing and obeying God's Word is the key to intimacy
with Jesus: Luke 8:21; cf. John 15:7.

Questions

1. How could you make use of the Old Testament in
   explaining the gospel to a friend?
2. Do you think we should focus on the Old Testament in
   our personal study and group discussion more than we
   do? Why, or why not?

4

So what's in it for me? I'm New Testament!

Now that's a sensible, understandable point of view, isn't it? Even if the wholeness and unity of the Bible are all we have tried to see, even if we ought to drill ourselves to think in terms of 'one Bible', not 'two Testaments', yet surely there is a dividing line somewhere, isn't there? Isn't there a difference between living with Malachi and living with Matthew? So why can't we just cut our losses, and concentrate on the twenty-seven books that make up the new covenant Scripture?

The two-act play

We've already looked at much of the answer to that question. We have seen how the whole Bible is one book, bound together by God's covenant promise (see Chapter 1). In Old and New Testaments alike, there is only one way of salvation: the way of faith in the Word God has spoken, the lamb of God and Jesus the Lamb. Furthermore, we learned that it is wrong and misleading to identify the Old Testament with law, and the New Testament with grace. Grace is grace and law is law, right through the Bible, and to those chosen and touched by his grace, God gives his law as the pattern of life which delights him (see Chapter 2). And in Chapter 3 we saw how the whole Bible is really about Jesus. It is his book; he is its overarching, unifying subject, and it is from his hands that we receive it and revere it as the Word of God.

Nevertheless, the Bible reached its wholeness in two

steps or stages, and one of the most helpful ways in which this has been expressed is to think of the two 'Testaments' as Act 1 and Act 2 of a two-act play. If we only had Act 1 we would say, 'Yes, that's fine – as far as it goes! But what comes next? Where is it all going? Were the promises kept – and how? What became of these great characters and stirring promises? There must be more!' And if we only had Act 2, we would say, 'Yes, that's fine, but it's all a bit impromptu! We are dropped into the middle of something, but not told what. We meet people but we don't know who they are. This Jesus, with his immense claims, comes on the scene just like that! Words and ideas are used but never explained. In fact, it's all very mysterious!' The first chapter of Matthew would be enough to stop us in our tracks. Jesus, says Matthew, did not 'begin' with Mary and Bethlehem, but with people called David and Abraham. But who, for pity's sake, are they?

But when we put the two acts together, we find that Act 1 prepares for, leads into, and is explained by Act 2. Act 2 emerges (as neat as you please) from Act 1, fulfils its promises and brings them to the outcome that was always intended. At the same time, the words and ideas in Act 2 are now clear, because they originated and, indeed, were explained in Act 1.

The ground we have covered in the preceding four chapters allows us to see how exact it is to think of the Bible in this way: not two 'testaments', but two 'acts' in one 'play'.

But there is more – a further and most important piece to drop into place.

My book

The title of this present chapter asks a question: What's in it for me? When I read the Old Testament, am I learning about bygone events which affected some unrelated people? Am I reading, at second hand, what is really someone else's book? Or is it in some sense 'my book'? And if so, in what ways?

It often helps to have a picture in mind, so here is a 'pictorial question'. Think of the Old Testament as a straight line. It begins with Adam, extends through Abraham, Moses, David and the line of kings, then on to the end of the monarchy, the Babylonian exile and the return home. On our line there are also appropriate points for the prophets. Now for the key question: where is the line going next? Not only the 'model' of the two-act play but also all the evidence which supports that model shouts out the answer: the straight line out of the Old Testament runs unbroken into the New – and nowhere else. Anything else which might think of itself as the prolongation of the Old Testament, or its successor, or lay claim to its inheritance, is no more than a cul-de-sac.

A case in point

The picture of the straight line is simply one way of representing the idea of 'fulfilment'. Jesus, describing the Old Testament comprehensively as 'the law and the prophets', said that he had not come 'to abolish [demolish], but to fulfil' (Matthew 5:17). What did he mean? To 'fulfil' means 'to give something that full and final form which was present and intended from the beginning'. There are two parts to this definition and both are important: first, earlier expressions of truth are given their final expression, so there is nothing more to be said or done. For example, all that the prophets foretold about the Messiah is at last perfectly expressed in Jesus (Hebrews 1:1). But, secondly, this fulfilment does not distort what was promised. It may be an outcome which was not, or even could not, be expected, but it is a perfect 'fit'. It does not twist or adapt what went before; it does not require special pleading or re-thinking. It is what was there and what was intended from the start. Carpenters will understand when I say that every piece of wood 'runs out' into its own appropriate 'end grain'. The end grain was there from the start but cannot be seen until the end. Gardeners will understand when I say that a perennial will bloom in its first year but may not come to perfection till year five. Nevertheless, the perfection, though it transcends the earlier blossoming, is what was there from the start. It is the natural and intended full and perfect expression.

The sacrifices

So it is, when the sacrifices commanded in the Old Testament achieve their full and final expression at Calvary, in the death of the Lord Jesus Christ. The whole of the Epistle to the Hebrews justifies saying this, but particularly that matchless chapter 10. The inability of animal blood to take away sin (verses 1–4) is explained (verses 5–9) by the fact that no animal could ever be a consciously and deliberately willing victim, like Jesus was. No animal could ever say, as he did (Matthew 26:39), 'I have come to do your will' (Hebrews 10:7). This means that, at best, an animal can only illustrate what it means to be a substitute, dying in the sinner's place, for it leaves the sinner unrepresented at the very heart of the matter – the rebellious will. But Jesus is different. Of him, Hebrews 10 can say (verse 12) that he offered 'for all time one sacrifice for sins', in total obedience to the will of the Father (verse 10), and in a way vouched for by the Holy Spirit (verses 15–18).

Yet what Jesus did can be called a 'sacrifice and offering' (verse 5), a burnt offering and a sin offering (verse 6). What he did was the essential, full, final and intended expression of the truth that the earlier sacrifices foreshadowed.

We will say much more later on this topic of Jesus and the sacrifices. New Testament fulfilments are the intended, full expression of Old Testament ideas, truths and foreshadowings.

The Old Testament: my pre-history, my expectation

We can now attempt to answer the question: what's in it for me? Our answer comes under three headings:

1. Those who believe in Jesus are the 'children of Abraham' (Galatians 3:7), 'the Israel of God' (6:16)

Paul's letter to the Galatians, from chapter 3 onwards, is a key text on this theme, that the covenant promises the Lord made to Abraham and his 'seed' (descendants) now belong, directly and properly, to those who believe in Jesus. Jesus' people – the whole company of believers – possess by right the great name, Israel. We need to remember that from the start, the chosen line of Abraham's 'seed' did not include all who could claim descent from Abraham. To Abraham's own way of thinking, why should his son Ishmael not qualify (Genesis 17:18) as the bearer of the Lord's blessing? But this was not God's purpose in election (Romans 9:11). His call was to Isaac, not Ishmael, a fact that Paul generalized in a daring and striking way: 'Not because they are his descendants are they all Abraham's children … It is not the natural children who are God's children, but the children of promise who are regarded as Abraham's offspring' (Romans 9:7–8). In this significant passage 'Abraham's children' and 'God's children' are the same people. Or, as Galatians 3:26–29 puts it, 'You are all sons of God through faith in Christ Jesus … If you belong to Christ, then you are Abraham's seed, and heirs according to the promise.'

That master teller of pulpit anecdotes, Bishop Maurice Wood, told of a Frenchman who had become a naturalized Englishman. When he was asked what difference this made, he replied, 'Oh, now I won the Battle of Waterloo!' Likewise, Christians can say, 'When we were redeemed from Egypt', for everything the Old Testament contains concerns Israel, and we are Israel.

2. Those who believe in Jesus are citizens of Zion

Read Psalm 87. It is a visionary meditation about Zion. This is the city the Lord loves (verse 2) and, in its ideal reality, it is a glorious place (verse 3). But it is also the focal point of the Lord's worldwide people. Rahab (Egypt) and Babylon (the great oppressors), Philistia (the feared adversary), Tyre in the far north and Cush in the remote south, can somehow claim a birthright in Zion (verse 4). This is the Zion the Lord will yet establish (verse 5), a 'world-city whose citizenship roll will include all who can claim to be born there' (verse 6). It is into this vision that Christian believers fit. To us, there is the 'Zion of the past', the city which was the focal point of our Old Testament pre-history. There is also the 'Zion yet to come', the heavenly Zion which will descend from God as a bride dressed for her husband (Revelation 21:2), the eternal dwelling of God and his people, the city into which nothing impure can enter, whose citizenship roll is 'the Lamb's book of life' (Revelation 5:1, 7; 21:27). But there is also the 'Zion of the here and now', the place of our present citizenship as those who believe in Jesus and await his appearance (Philippians 3:20), the Zion to which we have already come (Hebrews 12:22–24) and where all the blessings of God in Christ are already ours.

But if Zion is our city, then that Zion-dominated book, the Old Testament, is our book. It records our history and lays the groundwork of our eternal hope.

3. Those who believe in Jesus are the inheritors of the promised kingdom, where he is King

The idea of a kingdom is present in the Bible from the very start. Adam and Ishshah (Genesis 2:23; she was not 'Eve' till after the fall, 3:20) were co-regents of the whole earth (1:28), but, more explicitly, Abraham was promised royal descendants (17:6), and the Lord's covenant-promise to him had a territorial component (17:8).

Royal possession of the land of Canaan did not come about until the time of David. Even then, however, it was short-lived, for, after the eighty years of David and Solomon (1 Kings 2:10; 11:42), the inept Rehoboam brought about the division of the land into two uneasy and unsatisfactory kingdoms. But the hope and vision not only remained but grew in glory and importance, along with the expectation of a second David, the messianic King who would rule the whole world in an everlasting reign. Passages like Psalms 2, 72, or 89:19–29 reveal how the great hope remained and flourished. When the prophets took up this theme, they naturally expressed it in the territorial terms available to them.

When Isaiah (e.g. chapter 60) depicted the coming glory, envisaging his people in far-off exile, how could they have understood his words except in relation to the return home for which they waited? This would match the spirit of expectancy which fills the Old Testament: every next child would be the promised 'seed' (Genesis 3:15), every next king would be the Messiah, every next prophet would be the 'prophet like Moses' (Deuteronomy 18:15), every next disaster would be the onset of 'the Day of the Lord', and the return home would be the fulfilment of what Isaiah and others had forecast. But it was not so. The books of Ezra and Nehemiah describe a hard-pressed and minute community, harassed by influential neighbours, dominated by the far-off kings of Persia: no David, no glory, and for long enough, no House of the Lord, even. So off went Isaiah's great vision into the future, for it was God's Word and must come about in God's time.

But indeed, if they had attended more closely to what the prophets had actually foretold, they could have known that something greater must be in store than the throne of David as they had once known it, and the tiny land he had once ruled. For Isaiah (to go no further) not only envisaged a glory that the geographical Canaan could not contain but linked his kingdom expectations to God's creation of a new heaven and a new earth (Isaiah 65:17–25), marked by features which no mere worldly kingdom, however noble, could display, and which no mere human king could achieve (11:1–9).

Thus the Old Testament sets the scene for yet another 'So what?', and the New Testament alone provides the answer: Jesus came preaching the kingdom of God (Mark 1:14). Still, of course, people all around him were woodenly thinking in terms of a throne up the road in Jerusalem, and a son of David on that throne (e.g. Luke 19:11). For starters at least, the miniscule kingdom of the past would be replicated, and the Romans would be driven into the sea, as a preliminary to ultimate world dominion. Even after Jesus' death and resurrection, the apostles themselves were still thinking along this track (Acts 1:6). Jesus, however, had said something different to Pilate. Up before the Governor on the treasonable charge of being a king and wanting a kingdom, he was asked, 'Are you the king of the Jews?' He gave a most significant reply: 'My kingdom is not of this world. If it were, my servants would fight to prevent my arrest by the Jews. But now my kingdom is from another place … I am a king. In fact, for this reason I was born, and for this I came into the world, to testify to the truth. Everyone on the side of truth listens to me' (John 18:33–37).

A different kingdom

There it is, then: a kingdom not modelled on this world's ideas of kingliness and kingdom boundaries, but a kingdom originating in heaven; a kingdom enjoyed not by right of birth and not limited by tests of nationality; a kingdom not of visible boundaries and customs-posts and armed forces, but of choice and commitment to the truth, open to all who are enrolled in the service of Jesus and who believe the truth, as the truth is in Jesus (Ephesians 4:21) This is God's intended transnational, spiritual, alternative society, the kingdom and church of his Son (Colossians 1:13–14). To decribe the kingdom in these terms is no more of a distortion of Old Testament thinking than it is to see the animal sacrifices of the Old Testament as transcended and finished at Calvary. The cross of Christ was what the sacrifices had always pointed towards, and the heavenly kingdom of Jesus is what Canaan was always intended to become. This is not a contradiction, nor even an adjustment, but a biblical fulfilment.

In all these ways, and indeed in every way, the Old Testament is my book, my inheritance in Christ.

Following the straight line

The theme of this chapter can be put this way: walk straight out of the Old Testament, and where do we arrive? Unless we misread the map, take a false turning up a cul-de-sac, there is only one destination: the New Testament. Think about this for seven days:

Day 1
The promised 'seed': Genesis 3:15; Isaiah 7:14; Matthew 1:18–23; Galatians 4:4–5; Revelation 12:1–5.

Day 2
The family of Abraham: Genesis 17:7; 22:18; Deuteronomy 4:37; Matthew 3:9; Romans 9:6–7; Galatians 3:6–9, 26–29.

Day 3
David: 2 Samuel 7:11b–16; Psalms 2:4–12; 89:3–4, 19–29; Isaiah 11:1–3, 6–9; Ezekiel 34:22–24; Luke 1:30–33.

Day 4
Jerusalem/Zion: Deuteronomy 12:10–11; 1 Kings 8:11; Psalms 48:1–3, 12–14; 87:1–7; Isaiah 12; 25:6–9; 26:1–4; Hebrews 12:22–24; Revelation 22:1–5.

Day 5
The kingdom: Genesis 1:28; 15:18–21; 1 Kings 4:21; Psalm 72:8–11; Daniel 2:44; Matthew 4:17; 6:10; Luke 22:29; John 18:36–38; 1 Corinthians 15:50–54; Hebrews 12:28; Revelation 11:15.

Day 6
Atonement: Genesis 22:13; Exodus 12:12–13; Leviticus 17:11; Isaiah 53:4–6, 11; John 1:29, 35; Romans 3:24–25 (better in NKJV, ESV); Hebrews 10:1–14.

Day 7
The new heaven and the new earth: Isaiah 11:6–9; 65:17–25; 66:22; 2 Peter 3:13–14; Revelation 21:1–8.

So what's in it for me? I'm New Testament!

Questions

What difference does it make to you to know you are
   a. a child of Abraham?
   b. a citizen of Zion?
   c. an inheritor of the promised kingdom?
In light of this how would you share the gospel of Jesus
with someone who is Jewish?

PART TWO

Come for a walk through the Old Testament

No-hopers and their persistent God:

Genesis 12 – Deuteronomy 34

More than any other book in the world, it is true of the Bible that the more we know the whole, the more we understand the part. The same principle applies, of course, to individual books of the Bible. How often we know a bit here and a passage there, but we have no notion of how they fit into an overall plan We can name and admire individual trees but know little about the wood they are in.

What we want to do now, for the first five books of the Bible (known as the Pentateuch), is to survey the whole of this particular 'wood', and set up signposts here and there, in the hope of making it more meaningful as a whole, and less puzzling in its details.

Two unequal parts

The Pentateuch falls into two very unequal parts. Genesis 1 – 11 has the whole world as its theme: creation (1:1 – 2:4), the beginnings of human life, the first man and woman, Adam and Ishshah (1:1 – 2:24), the entrance of sin (chapter 3), sin's disastrous consequences (4:1 – 6:4), God's wrathful reaction in the universal flood (6:5 – 9:17), the re-inhabited world (9:18 – 10:32), and the divine judgment of universal disunity at Babel (11:1–9). Everything is told in a universal way. Even when an incident happens in a single place – such as, for example, the building of the tower in

Shinar (11:1ff.) – there are universal implications and the destiny of the whole world is at stake.

How very different is the scene we enter in Genesis 12. The genealogy (11:10–26) 'spans' from Noah's son, Shem, to the birth of a single individual, Abram. Suddenly the world seems almost empty! Abraham occasionally meets someone outside his own entourage (Pharaoh, 12:15ff.; four kings, 14:1ff.; Abimelech, 20:1ff.), but overall we have the impression of an individual living as a nomad in an empty landscape. The actual situation, as our imagination would tell us and as archaeology confirms, was very different. Canaan was swarming with people; the world was seething with activity. But of all of this the book of Genesis tells us next to nothing. It concerns itself exclusively with this one man and his family.

The same remains true right to the end of Deuteronomy. Abram became Abraham (Genesis 17:5), and his family increased. Its twelve-tribe population grew to the extent that it seemed to threaten the well-being of Egypt (Exodus 1:8ff.). Its armies could defeat the Amalekites (Exodus 17:1ff.) and even the more considerable powers of Sihon and Og in Transjordan (Deuteronomy 2:26 – 3:17). Yet, at the same time, Israel seems strangely isolated, and a single individual, Moses, dominates the story for four whole books, from Exodus to Deuteronomy. Of the world around we learn nothing. Israel is the whole story.

Up to this point, then, the Pentateuch looks like this:

Genesis 1 – 11	Genesis 12 – Deuteronomy 34
Universal	Particular

When we turn to examine the second and longer section of the Pentateuch, we find that it also falls into two parts:

Genesis 12 to Exodus 24

These chapters trace the story of the Lord's people from Abraham (Genesis 12 – 25), through Isaac (Genesis 25 –

27), Jacob (Genesis 28 – 50), the birth of his twelve sons, (Genesis 29 – 30), Joseph (Genesis 39ff), Israel in Egypt (Exodus 1), Moses (Exodus. 2ff.), the sequence of events leading up to the departure from Egypt (Exodus 3 – 14), the wilderness journey to Sinai (Exodus 18), and the giving of the law (Exodus 19 – 24).

But Bible history is never the mere recital of facts, never simply 'one thing after another'. There is always a story-within-the-story, some revealed truth about God and his dealings with his world, enshrined in the recorded events. In Genesis 12 – Exodus 24, the 'real' story is that God promoted a relationship (a covenant) between himself and one man (Abram) and, through that one man, with his descendants or 'seed'. The story is bracketed by the formal inauguration of the covenant (Genesis 15) and its solemn ratification (Exodus 24).

It is all carefully told in an orderly fashion. We can picture it as a landscape with twin mountain peaks in the foreground and a matching set of twin peaks in the distance. The first pair is made up of Genesis 15, where the covenant was inaugurated by sacrifice, and Genesis 17, where the terms of life within the covenant are sketched in the law of perfection (verse 2) and the rite of circumcision (verses 9–14). In other words, there is the mountain peak of covenant making, or of sacrifice, followed by the mountain peak of covenant living, or of law. The second, distant pair of peaks shows the same pattern. In Exodus 12, God's covenant activity in Egypt (cf. 2:24ff.) is consummated by the Passover sacrifice, and in Exodus 20 – 23 the terms of life within the covenant are spelled out in the Ten Commandments and their related laws. So here again we have the mountain of covenant making (or sacrifice) and the mountain of covenant living, with the broad commandment of perfection (Genesis 17:1) expanded into detailed laws covering all of life.

All this material is linked by a telling symbol of God's presence with his people. Jeremiah 34:18 helps us to understand the (to our eyes) strange ceremony of Genesis 15:9–10, 17: the severed carcases and the path made by the two halves. It was a very solemn way of making and confirming an oath. To walk this pathway carried the implication: 'So let it be done to me if I break this undertaking' (cf. 1 Samuel 1:7). In this way the Lord made and ratified his covenant-promise, and the symbol which represented his presence was (literally, Genesis 15:17) 'an oven with smoke and fiery flame'. Nomads used an earthenware oven for cooking. It was heated by being filled with combustible material which was then fired. Smoke and flame belched out, leaving the oven at the necessary temperature. In this smoke and flame, the Lord signalled his presence as the covenant God.

It was in the same way that he accompanied his redeemed pilgrims out of Egypt (Exodus 13:21–22; 40:36–38). Indeed, in their moment of dire need by the Red Sea (14:9), the great pillar of cloud and fire moved to stand protectively between them and their foes, the only occasion when the pillar deserted its leading position to became a rear-guard! But the covenant God of cloud and fire was climactically seen when Mount Sinai was completely shrouded in smoke, because the Lord descended upon it in fire (20:18). What began awesomely yet unpretentiously in the presence of a single human observer, was consummated for the whole redeemed people: the Lord was really present in all his holiness (fire), yet graciously shrouded himself with a cloud, thus 'accommodating' his holiness to dwell among sinners (but not changing or diminishing it).

We can now pause again and try to represent the Pentateuch from Genesis 12 onwards in a diagram:

Covenant sacrifice / Covenant law		Covenant sacrifice / Covenant law	
Gen. 15	Gen. 17	Exod. 12	Exod. 20ff.

Exodus 25 to Deuteronomy 34

Outwardly, the story is continued, from the time they left Sinai to the moment when the people are finally poised to enter the Promised Land. Exodus 25 – 40 and the whole of Leviticus are concerned with the setting up of the tabernacle and the religious duties associated with it. Numbers records the journey on to Canaan, focusing especially on the people's faithless refusal to enter the Promised Land when they reached it for the first time, and how they were condemned to fritter away a whole generation in the wilderness (Numbers 13 – 14). The book of Deuteronomy takes place on the very border of Canaan (cf. Deuteronomy 1:1), where Moses, himself forbidden to enter (1:37ff.; 3:23ff.; 4:21ff.; 32:48ff.; 34:1ff.), gave his people some final moral and spiritual instruction for the life that would be theirs when eventually they would possess their promised inheritance.

But, once again, the 'meat' of Exodus 25 to Deuteronomy 34 is the inner story: the story of fellowship with God within the covenant.

The sacrifices

The first in each pair of 'mountain-peaks' in our first diagram was concerned with the theme of covenant-sacrifice. This theme is taken up and completed in Exodus 25 to Leviticus 27. The people entered into the covenant by blood-sacrifice and they can only continue in fellowship with their covenant God if sacrificial blood is available to maintain the relationship intact. For this purpose, the Lord mercifully established a system of sacrifices centring on the great Tent where he dwells in the midst of his people (cf. Exodus 29:43–46). The repeated sacrifices of Leviticus preserve the covenant and the people of the covenant, and make it safe for them to be in the presence of their holy God.

The law

The second mountain peaks in each pair were concerned with the laws for life within the covenant. This theme is completed in Deuteronomy, Moses' own exposition of the law. He started by reviewing the history of his people from the time they left Sinai to their present moment, when they were poised to inherit (Deuteronomy 1 – 4); then he turned to expound and explain the law God had given through him. Chapter 5 tells how the Ten Words or Commandments were given. Chapters 6 – 13 deal with the implications of Commandments 1–4, dwelling particularly on the First Commandment, and what it means to be devoted to the one and only God. Chapters 14 – 26 offer a broad review of the rest of the law of Moses, explaining, elaborating and applying it. Chapters 27 – 30 look forward specifically to life in the Promised Land: how the law is to be made central to the life of the people by being identified with the mountains of Ebal and Gerizim (chapter 27); how obedience is the key to prosperity (chapters 28 – 29); how the people are faced with the choice between life and death (chapter 30). The remainder of the book records the final acts of Moses, ending with a postscript (chapter 34) narrating his death.

So Exodus 12 onwards, then, looks like this:

Covenant sacrifice Exod. 12	Covenant law Exod. 19 – 24	Covenant sacrifice Exod. 25 – Leviticus	Covenant law Deut.

The book of Numbers

We see, then, that there is an impressive unity about Genesis 12 to Deuteronomy 34. But how does the book of Numbers fit into it?

Numbers is a prime example of the way the Bible writes history. It covers forty years but tells of only three episodes. The mere amassing of facts does not interest the Old Testament historian: if the moral and spiritual temperature can be taken by three events, what need is there to record more? If the theological lessons are fully covered and the Lord is truly revealed in three events, then to want more is only to burden the mind with needless detail, and to confuse information with knowledge.

Three things tell all we need to know about the forty

years between Sinai and Canaan. Firstly, there is the episode of the spies (Numbers 13 – 14). Hitherto it has proved enough that God has gone before his people (cf. 10:33–36), but now an element of faithlessness enters, and God's providential care of his people is seemingly doubted. The second episode is the rebellion (Numbers 16 – 17) of Korah, Dathan and Abiram against the authority of Moses and Aaron. As the events showed, this was a rejection of the means of government and leadership which the Lord had appointed. The spy episode questioned his providence governing the future; the rebellion episode set aside his rule over the present. The third event on which Numbers dwells is the threat imposed by the seer, Balaam, who had been called to curse Israel (Numbers 22 – 24). This was a real danger (cf. 22:6b), and one of which Israel was ignorant, and could therefore do nothing to counteract. But no danger is hidden from the Lord, and he guarded his people from a dire threat of which they were blissfully unaware.

A great truth

One continuing lesson is clear: the covenant people can never, of themselves, inherit the blessings of the covenant. Their own faithlessness and rebelliousness, and also the forces ranged against them, will keep them out of Canaan. But they are not left to themselves! On their side is the covenant God who remains faithful throughout their unfaithfulness, and will never change his purposes or his promises. Numbers 14, recording their faithless refusal to enter and take possession, is followed by chapter 15 (note especially verses 2, 18) which calmly affirms that, nonetheless, the Land will yet be possessed. Numbers 16 records rebellion against God's appointed priesthood, but chapters 17 and 18 quietly confirm Aaron and his priesthood. Numbers 22:6 (cf. Genesis 12:3) relates how an unknown but real supernatural threat hung over the people, and also challenged God's promises to Abram, but the Lord unobtrusively interposed his own power, ruling and overruling Balaam. The covenant stands only because the Lord is faithful to it; he guards his people even from dangers of which they are not aware, and they inherit only because he will bring them into their inheritance.

In all this, the book of Numbers matches the historical material in Genesis 18 to Exodus 1. Human failure, hostile circumstances, and enemy action threaten the covenant people, and if they were left to themselves they would lose their crown, but they are never left alone. It would be a fine exercise to read these chapters simply to underline the element of divine oversight and providential provision and care.

Whether in high points like Genesis 22:1–16 or low failures like Genesis 12:10–20, sad wrongdoing (Genesis 37:23), false imprisonment (Genesis 39:20), famine (Genesis 45:4–7), even threatened genocide (Exodus 1) – whatever the case, Joseph found that the Lord was with him. Jacob can look back and speak of the God who was his shepherd (Genesis 48:15), and even the superpower of Pharaoh finds itself foiled at every turn (Exodus 1:11–12, 15–17; 1:22 – 2:10). When Jacob took the hazardous road to Egypt, it was with the promise in his ears that 'I will go down to Egypt with you, and I will surely bring you back again' (Genesis 46:4). And, at grass-roots level, the misused Hagar was met in her need by the Angel who was none other than the Lord himself (Genesis 16:7, 13; 21:15–20).

The fuller pattern

This, then, is the point which our enquiry into the pattern and meaning of the first five books has reached:

(a)	(b)	(c)	(a)[1]	(b)[1]	(a)[2]	(c)[1]	(b)[2]
Cov. sac. Gen. 15	Cov. law Gen. 17	God's care Gen. 18 - Exod. 1	Cov. sac. Exod. 12	Cov. law Exod. 19 - 24	Sac. (elab.) Exod. 25 - Lev.	God's care Num.	Law (elab.) Deut.

The (a) portions (the sacrifices) establish the *basis of fellowship* with God. This is not explained in Genesis, but is made clear by the Passover narrative (Exodus 12) and by later teaching in Exodus and Leviticus (e.g. Leviticus 17:11). It is only through the shed blood of a divinely authorized sacrifice that we can approach the holy God, remain in his fellowship, and be safe.

The (b) portions set out the *pattern of life* for those who have been brought under the divine covenant promise: not how to get there but how to live as those who have already been redeemed. This is the way Paul put it when he wrote to the Colossians: first, 'we pray for you because we have heard of your faith'; then, 'we have not stopped praying for you and asking God to fill you with the knowledge of his will'; and finally, 'we pray this in order that you may live a life worthy of the Lord, and may please him' (Colossians 1:3, 9–10). Saved by faith, we long to live so as to please our Saviour God. And this is why he gives us his law.

The (c) portions take us 'behind the scenes'. Left to ourselves, we cannot but fall, and fail, and stop short, but God is on our side. Those he has brought to himself he will also preserve for himself, and he will fulfil every purpose of his will for them. When we come to him, by grace, through faith, we come under his ever-persistent providential care.

A verse a day for seven days from Deuteronomy

Apart from the Psalms, there is no book which so fully sums up what the Old Testament is 'all about' as Deuteronomy. It's better to read it right through, of course, but, for starters, here are seven typical 'tasters':

Day 1
1:18: Every part of life must be brought under the Word of God.

Day 2
4:6: Obedience to God's Word is our primary testimony to the world.

Day 3
8:2–3: The trials of life – where they come from, what they are all about.

Day 4
10:12–13: Five great verbs: fear, walk, love, serve, observe.

Day 5
20:1, 4: The God of the past, the present and the future.

Day 6
30:19–20: Ours is a life of ceaseless choice.

Day 7
33:26–27, 29: Incomparable God, unfailing security, blessed people.

Questions

1. The teaching of the Pentateuch can be tough for modern readers to get to grips with. Identify any parts that remain baffling to you. Discuss these in your group. How can you help each other with your questions? If you are studying alone, keep a note of your questions and find ways to explore some answers (the booklist at the back may help).
2. How have you experienced the God of the past, present and future
   a. as a church?
   b. as an individual?
   Reflect and be thankful.

The whole world not forgotten:

Genesis 1 – 11

We must now step back into the shorter opening section of the Pentateuch, the eleven chapters with worldwide themes, with which Genesis opens. As with all Bible history-writing, we are not told everything we might wish to know, but only what we need to know. The narrative fixes our attention on three typical events: the fall (Genesis 3 – 6), the flood (6 – 9) and the scattering (11:1–9). They are all stories of loss: how mankind, by sin, lost its home in God's Garden, brought destruction on his world, and shattered human fellowship. Each loss found us blameworthy and brought us under divine judgment, but each time judgment was inexplicably mingled with mercy.

God is still on the throne

The theme of these chapters is not really the world at all, but the sovereignty of God over the world. It is one of their most striking features that when, in Genesis 3, the great rebellion has taken place and mankind, in the individual Adam, has made its bid to be 'like God', the Lord God steps into the Garden with his sovereignty unimpaired. The once voluble serpent is now silent, and neither the rebellious human pair nor anything else in all creation can resist the sovereign will which decrees a curse upon a world of sinners (3:14–19). Yet the curse is not the whole story.

The edict of death and the promise of life

The law of the Garden had insisted (2:16–17) that the wages of sin would be death, yet humankind lives on. To be sure, they now live outside the Garden, for they have lost their privileged place and no longer enjoy peace with God. Nevertheless they live on. The Sovereign Lord has in some sense deferred the edict of death, because he purposes to bring to birth one born to a woman who will undo all that the serpent has accomplished and will bring its time of usurping to an end (3:15). The very moment of sin became the moment of promise. No sooner did mankind fall into sin than the Lord God forecast the birth of the Saviour!

These early chapters of Genesis present as great a challenge to our powers of interpretation as anything in the whole Bible. There are always further dimensions to be explored. The Bible itself is a 'great deep', but it is at its deepest in these seeming (and in one sense, actual) simplicities. So, Genesis 2:17 warns of the sentence of death, but 3:15 indicates that life goes on. Yet that is not the whole story. In the Bible death is never the end. Physical death is a change of place (earth is left for Sheol, the place where the dead live on), a change of state (the body-soul unity of earthly life is sundered; the body falls into the ground; the soul lives on in Sheol). But one thing is not changed: there is *continuity of person*. Abraham is gathered to his people (Genesis 25:8); Jacob will see Joseph again (Genesis 37:35), and David his week-old baby boy (2 Samuel 12:23).

So Adam and Eve did die, though not physically. They experienced a change of place: the outside world instead of the Garden; a change of state: distance from God instead of wonderful fellowship. But they were still Adam and Eve, and still all too really carried the burden and consequence of their guilt.

When we see things in this light, then the mercy which put the edict of death in abeyance and voiced the promise of life is mercy indeed.

Universal wickedness and saving grace

The flood too would seem to be the moment when wrath will overtake a whole world of sinners. In Genesis 6:5–7 the repeated word 'man/humankind' is impressive: the whole race is reviewed and nothing but wickedness is found (verse 5); in the whole race there is not one single person who does not cause grief and regret to the Lord (verse 6); and (verse 7) the whole race without exception is doomed. Humankind, unfit to live in God's Garden, is not even fit to remain in God's world. How impressive is the sovereignty, then, that can weigh up a whole world, pronounce sentence, and know that no opposition can be raised. But how much more movingly impressive is the grace that rides on the clouds of wrath to reach, touch and save Noah! Noah was, as the hymn says, 'a debtor to mercy alone'. Noah found grace (Genesis 6:8); grace found Noah (see Chapter 1).

The word 'grace' (Hebrew *ḥēn*) has the same meaning or usage throughout the Bible, and is the equivalent of the Greek *charis*. It is not a boon which God imparts so much as a gift of himself. The grace of God is God being gracious, that is to say, freely reaching out in goodness, mercy and forgiveness to those undeserving of God's goodness. Grace is a self-imposed activity, undertaken by God at the sole prompting of his own heart, and bestowed on those to whom he chooses to be gracious, for reasons which make sense to him and are not disclosed to us. God chose, in a world of sinners, to save some. 'But why, if he is gracious, did he not save all?' cries the thoughtless critic, and the Bible replies, 'Be astonished that he should save any! Marvel at the inexplicable wonder of grace!'

Man's way of salvation, and God's

After the flood, the historian selects a typical event to illustrate the way things were. People, the would-be authors of their own safety, security and community (Genesis 11:1–9), arrive at a moment of technological advance – the discovery of how to make bricks and mortar (verse 3). The fact that they are no longer dependent on finding building materials to hand but can actually create what they need, suggested an answer to a pressing problem: how to achieve and maintain a cohesive and safe society which would be proof against those divisive tendencies which sinners find within themselves (verse 4), and which would leave scattered and small groups vulnerable to attack.

To build a tower reaching to heaven (verse 4) is not necessarily to entertain rebellious ambitions against God. It is rather a metaphor for walled strength (cf. Deuteronomy 1:28). It speaks of vaunting self-confidence that mankind can now, through technology and by his own abilities, solve his own problems. No longer dependent on God, mankind can well do without him. Who wants rocks when they can make their own bricks? But it is all a vain hope. They neither have the power to achieve their aims, nor does the Lord allow them to. They plan a tower to reach heaven, but (Genesis 11:5) the Lord had to come down before he could even see it. There is something more: in attempting to be the authors of their own salvation, they had in fact reached the point at which God always says 'No'. He will not ever allow self-salvation to succeed, and so they fell prey to the very thing from which they sought to save themselves. They feared dispersion, and the dreaded dispersion took place – coupled now with a second act of God's judgment, the irretrievable breakdown of communication (verses 8–9).

End and beginning

In this way the Lord drew a line under their technological salvation: 'they stopped building' (Genesis 11:8). But that was not the end of the story. Just as at the time of the fall, death was postponed by life (3:15), and at the time of the flood, God's grace interposed to save Noah (6:8) – so now, again, there will be a surprising mercy.

At first sight another genealogy, coming at Genesis 11:10, prompts us to groan. Another list of mostly unknown names. But look more carefully! It starts with the new beginning granted to Noah and his sons (11:10). It wends its way along a line of obscure names, until it ends with a man named Abram (11:26ff.), the one to whom God planned to say, 'and all peoples on earth will be blessed through you' (12:3). God never gives up. Outwardly the world is acting with that intense self-centredness and pride: 'nothing will be impossible for them which they plan to do' (11:6). But imperceptibly, behind the scenes of frenetic building, God's better plan is working its way forward: generation follows generation, unknown follows unknown, until the man of promise is born, in whom (12:3) and in whose seed (22:18) the universal blessedness which has been lost will be restored.

This is always one of the purposes of the genealogies which lie scattered through the Old Testament, and, indeed, of the one with which the New Testament opens its doors (Matthew 1). But where we are bored, we should rather be excited; where we soldier on through a list of unknown people, we should rather find God. This is the God who never gives up, never wearies or loses track of his plans as time passes. The river of his operations may disappear underground, but it is flowing forward, ready to surface again when what Paul calls 'the fullness of time' (Galatians 4:4, ESV) arrives. And with God's moment comes God's man, humanly speaking the product of interminable 'begets' and 'begottens', but more truly seen as a plan come to pass. Such a man was Abram, in whose person the section Genesis 12 – Deuteronomy 34 is cemented to Genesis 1 – 11.

Two bridges

1 The blessing is coming back

This, then, is how the two sections of the Pentateuch belong together. God separated this one man, Abram, and his descendants, not only for their benefit alone but also for the world's blessing, to retrieve the blessings that had been forfeited.

First, at the fall Adam lost peace with God (Genesis 3:8), and was banished from the Garden (3:24ff.). Secondly,

Genesis 4 – 6 records how, outside the Garden, sin increased and spread, bringing divine wrath, expressed in judgment and death (6 – 9). Thirdly, the blessing of peace between people in a harmonious, cohesive and safe human society was lost when human do-it-yourself arrogance provoked the scattering at Babel, and the confusion of languages made human divisions permanent (11:9).

In Abram, however, the lost blessings are on their way back. In Genesis 22:18, 'will be blessed' is actually a reflexive form of the verb – 'will bless themselves' or, in context, 'will find the blessing they need'. Here indeed is the good news for ancient man! In Abraham and his seed all the families of the earth will recover the blessedness which has been lost. The Lord intends to destroy Satan and all his works so that peace with God will come back, there will yet be a saving grace whereby divine judgment will be satisfied, and the universal wickedness and doom of sin will be countered. Divisions and divisiveness will cease in the City of God that is yet to be. The world is indeed lost in sin and death, but not forgotten by the ever-merciful, ever-saving God.

2 The covenant-making God

But how? We saw that the story of Abraham and his family was inwardly the story of the establishing and implementing of the covenant. When the covenant reached its mature form, it involved God reaching down into the world, making a choice among all the people in Egypt, and bringing out those whom he chose, redeemed by the blood of the lamb. This, in principle, is exactly what God did individually for Noah at the time of the flood when the word 'covenant' appeared in Scripture for the first time (Genesis 6:18). The covenant theme bridges the two sections of the Pentateuch, not simply as a word which occurs in each, but as the way in which the same God plans to restore blessing to the whole world: selecting, saving and preserving a people for himself. This is what the Pentateuch is all about: the record of blessing lost and the divine purpose of blessing restored. This is why it is one book much more than it is five. But then, this too is what the whole Bible is about, and why it is one book much more than it is sixty-six books, or even two testaments!

Genesis 1 – 3 in seven days

Day 1
1:1–13: What was done each day? What picture of God the Creator emerges?

Day 2
1:13–25: How do the second three days match the first three? How many times does Genesis 1 say that the creation was good? What does 'good' mean?

Day 3
1:26 – 2:3: List the things that are special and different about humankind.

Day 4
2:4–17: In verse 4, 'account' (*tôlĕdōt*) means 'subsequent/ongoing history'. We move here from the majestic account of God's creative work (1:1 – 2:3) to the beginnings of human life on earth. What responsibilities, privileges and duties did the Lord God give the man?

Day 5
2:18–24: What do you reckon is the lesson to learn from verses 19–20? What does this passage teach about marriage?

Day 6
3:1–12: Looking at the ways in which the woman was enticed into sin, what can we learn about resisting temptation?

Day 7
3:13–24: The consequences of Adam's sin are still with us – indeed, they are part of our nature. How many consequences can you find here?

'He's the image of his Father!'

Yes, we can hear kindly aunts cooing over the new baby, or, depending on what they think of the father, perhaps their hearts are full of pity rather than kindness! But, aside from that, to reflect the image of our Father is (are you surprised?) the great purpose behind all the laws that came through Moses.

Living in God's church

We must start, however, with a brief reminder of the ground covered in Chapter 3. The truest window we possess into the mind and life of Old Testament believers is the book of Psalms. Here we meet the saints of the old covenant in their joys and sorrows. Here we feel the weight of their problems and covet the richness of their knowledge and love of God. Spiritual life under the old covenant, with all its laws, was far from being dull drudgery.

Here are some verses (almost at random) from Psalm 119: God's law was a delight (verse 92), an object of love (97), respected as truth (142), a means of peace (165) and (surprise, surprise!) a guarantee of liberty (45); it was a treasure above all earthly wealth (72). To say that we do not usually think of Old Testament law in these terms is an understatement indeed, but that's how things were for our spiritual relatives in ancient times.

Living in God's world

God's law has always been at the centre of his dealings with humans. In Genesis 2, Adam in the Garden was under God's law (verses 16–17), and only through obedience could he continue to enjoy the Garden's riches. Verses 16–17 contrast 'every tree', which is there for enjoyment, with one single tree, which is forbidden, yet that single tree tells us what God's law is all about.

Adam did not win his way into the Garden by keeping God's law. He was placed there by God's decision and goodness (Genesis 2:8). It was the divine provision, as we would say, of grace. It was God's gift to God's man. But, once inside the Garden, he continued to enjoy its blessings only by obedience to the law of the Garden. In this way, at the very start, the Bible marries two enduring partners – obedience and life. Obedience safeguarded the enjoyment of the life that was life indeed; disobedience not only forfeited that life but replaced it by death. With disobedience came the birth of a bad conscience (Genesis 3:8), the replacement of love with resentment (verse 12), the corruption of marriage (verse 16) and the dislocation of humans from their environment (verses 17–19), which now turns to fight against them, and only grudgingly provides a living.

The rest of the Old Testament perpetuates this view of humans in their environment: only by obedience to God's law can we live successfully and prosperously in God's world. Indeed, the very environment itself turns against the disobedient. The earth is defiled by law-breakers (Leviticus 18:24–30) and 'vomits out' (20:22) those who fail to keep the law. The created environment has what we might call a 'moral vitality' all its own, which makes it side with those who side with the Creator, and become the enemy of his foes. The reason for this is because it is the Spirit of God himself, the Holy Spirit, who operates in creation (Genesis 1:2; Psalm 33:6), and it is his activity which is seen in both the renewal and decay of nature (Psalm 104:30; Isaiah 40:7). Just as he is 'the Lord and Giver of life', so too he is the Lord and Giver of death. The life which vitalizes the environment is God's life, full of his holiness.

Thus the Old Testament has a distinct understanding of our environment, and at its centre lies the law of God the Creator.

The image of God

'Man', humankind, beginning with the creation of the first male and female, is the crown of the creative work of God. The threefold use of the verb 'to create' in Genesis 1:27 marks humans as both essentially creaturely and God's perfect creative act. This human uniqueness is summed up in the description, 'in our image, after our likeness'. Now, these words, respectively *ṣelem* and *dĕmût* in Hebrew, are used uniformly throughout the Old Testament of the outward form or shape of something or someone. This must be their leading idea in Genesis 1:26 also. This does not, of course, mean that visible form and shape are part of the divine essence: for God is Spirit (Isaiah 31:3; 1 John 3:24). Nonetheless, we find in the Old Testament (e.g. Judges 13:3, 6, 10, 15) that, when the Lord chose to show himself visibly to someone, their first impression was of meeting a 'man'. That is to say, there is an outward shape uniquely suited to (though not essential to) the divine perfection, and it was in that image and likeness that man was created.

But pretty well every aspect of human nature is related, directly or indirectly, in the Genesis narrative to the image of God.

Matrimonial
Genesis 1:26–27, but particularly 5:1–2, teach that the two, the man and woman, who become 'one flesh' (cf. 2:24) in marriage, are 'in the image of God'. In their togetherness they are called 'man', and in their togetherness the two become one and display the image of God.

Governmental

Dominion over the creation (Genesis 1:28) is vested, not in the male, Adam, but in the created pair together: 'God … said to them … Rule [a plural imperative] … over every living creature.' Ancient kings, so we learn, used to put images of themselves at the borders of their realms and in every place where they claimed lordship. This is probably what 1 Samuel 15:12 means. Humankind, in God's image, is God's vice-regent, his assertion of sovereignty over the whole creation.

Spiritual

Unlike the beasts, upon whom the Lord imposed his will simply by fact (Genesis 1:22), the man and woman (verse 28) are subject to a personal address by God. Genesis 1:22 is just 'God said', whereas verse 28 has 'said to them'.

Moral

Genesis 2:15–17: The beasts are left by their Creator to live out their instinctual life. This is the unthinking way in which they live so as to delight him. There is a lovely alternative translation for Psalm 104:26: 'which you formed to have fun with' (cf. ESV margin). But in the case of humankind, the Lord delights in our conscious moral obedience to his will. He addresses his word to us (Genesis 1:28) so that we may knowingly mould our lives according to it; he imposes his law upon us (2:16–17), and requires us to make choices in the light of consequences, good or evil.

Rational

In the wonderful parade of the beasts in Genesis 2:19–20, the Lord gives Adam the opportunity to exercise his rational powers, to arrange the beasts in categories, to associate male with female, to discern what is distinctive in each species and to allocate appropriate names. In the whole created world, humankind alone has this power of thoughtful observation, classification and reasoning.

In all these ways, the uniqueness of the divine image

permeates human nature. The image of God is not to be sought in this aspect of our nature or that, nor is it located here or there. It is what we are. It is the definition of what humankind truly is, and the truly human life is the life that lives out the divine image.

Another image of God

Leviticus 19, however, helps us to see that God has another image also. In this rather extraordinary chapter, every side of human experience is reviewed, and God's law is applied to it. The chapter insists and implies that there is nothing in our lives that is not subject to the rule of obedience: filial duty (verse 3); religious commitment (4); ritual (5–8); care of the needy (9–10) and disabled (14); honesty in deed and word (11); promise keeping (12); the integrity of the courts (15–16); secret animosity (17) and vengefulness (18); farming (19); dress (19); sexual misconduct (20) and much, much more! And it all seems such a muddle. There is no way of predicting what will come next. This is probably deliberate, for in life there is no way of predicting what will come next. Life itself is a muddle of all manner of things and all manner of surprises. But nothing lies outside our duty to God.

The great central truth of life

All this variety, however, rests on one foundation: 'I am the Lord' (e.g. verses 3, 10, 12; sixteen times in total). In this way the Lord claims all life as his, to be lived according to his requirements. But look carefully. In our English Bibles, 'Lord' is printed in upper-case letters: 'LORD'. This means that it represents 'Yahweh', the divine name, the 'I am what I am' of Exodus 3:14. The significance, then, of the recurring claim, 'I am the Lord', is not 'You must do what I tell you just because I tell you – I'm your Master!', but 'You must be what you must be because I am what I am.' In other words, every precept of the law, applied to every aspect of life, even in its minutiae, is a statement of what he is. His commandments are not arbitrary or random, but flow out of his character. *God's law is his character, expressed in commandments, so that, in obeying, we display his likeness, and live out our true nature.*

Humankind is the living, personal image of God; the law is the preceptual image of God, the image of God expressed in commandments. Leviticus 19 makes this clear from the outset: 'Be holy because I, the Lord your God, am holy' (verse 2). The Lord wants his people to live in his image, and to that end he has given them his law. The commands of God's law 'trigger' the image of God which is our essential nature.

A truly human life

There is a tremendously important conclusion to be drawn from all this: When humans in the image of God and law in the image of God come together in the obedient life, then humans are indeed 'being themselves'. This is what we were created to be; this is the distinctive and truly human life. Our nature is the image of God, and the law is given to activate and to direct that nature into a truly human life. Any other life, anything that flouts the law of God, is subhuman.

Of course, it is true that in a world of sinners the law, regrettably, has to give itself to the task of curbing and rebuking anti-social and degrading practices (cf. 1 Timothy 1:8–11), but God's law has, to a far greater extent, the function of liberating us to live according to our true nature.

The law that liberates

We saw that the law of God (Genesis 2:16–17) was Adam's key to the true liberty of the Garden, a liberty of situation. But the law of God liberates us in a more personal sense also. A girl in a television play, in that typical television drama state, a ten-years-of-marriage crisis, said, 'I'm gonna be myself, as soon as I've worked out what "myself" is!' The Bible is the only book that could give her an answer. Her 'self' is the 'image of God' – overlaid, it is true, by our sinfulness; defaced, corrupted, as far gone as possible in original sin; but still the divinely revealed and only true definition of what it is to be human. The law of God expresses his image in its commands. Every precept of the law reflects some essential of the divine nature. The Seventh Commandment, insisting on fidelity to the marriage covenant, arises from the truth that covenant-keeping is of the essence of his nature. The law of God is the true life of those created in the image of God.

When James (1:25; 2:12) speaks of Christians as bound by 'the law of liberty', he is of course referring, not narrowly to the law of Moses, but broadly to living according to 'the word' (1:21–22) or 'according to the Scripture' (2:8, NKJV). Psalm 119:45 says exactly the same: 'And I will walk hither and yon in a broad place, because it is your precise directions I am determined to seek' (author's translation). The verb 'to walk hither and yon' (from the Hebrew *hālak*) describes Abram enjoying unfettered liberty of movement in the Promised Land (Genesis 13:17). The 'broad place' is a picture of freedom, the opposite of cramped conditions (cf. the 'broad rivers' of Isaiah 33:21). 'Precise directions' is the noun *piqqûdîm*, expressing the most detailed, itemized application of God's law to human life. The verb 'to seek' is regularly used not of looking for something lost but of paying assiduous attention to something. In other words, the more closely and determinedly we tie ourselves to God's commands, the freer we become. The 'law of liberty' is the law that liberates because it is the expression of our true nature as the image of God. It is in obedience to him that we are most truly ourselves.

We would be silly to limit verses like Deuteronomy 4:1; 8:1; 30:19–20 to long life, or length of tenure. Rather, the Lord promises his people life that is life indeed (cf. John 10:10). Psalm 119:50, translated accurately, says it all: 'Your word has given me life' (NKJV).

The Lord Jesus Christ was the incarnate Image of God. To know, see, hear and watch him was to know, see, hear and watch the Father (John 14:7–11). He was also the ceaselessly and perfectly obedient One (8:29). Obedience and the image of God belong together.

A week with the Ten Commandments

Day 1
The First Commandment: sole loyalty to the only God: Exodus 20:3; Deuteronomy 4:39–40; 6:4–9; 10:20–21; Matthew 22:37–38.

Day 2
The Second Commandment: spiritual worship: Exodus 20:4–6; Deuteronomy 4:12; Psalm 51:15–17; John 4:23–24.

Day 3
The Third Commandment: holy reverence: Exodus 20:7; Leviticus 19:12; 24:10–16; Psalm 148:13; Matthew 6:9.

Day 4
The Fourth Commandment: our time is the Lord's: Exodus 20:8–11; Deuteronomy 4:12–16; Numbers 15:32–36; Isaiah 56:2, 4b–5; 58; Mark 2:23–28; Colossians 2:16.

Day 5
The Fifth Commandment: the God-given structure of home life: Exodus 20:12; Deuteronomy 5:16; Proverbs 4:1; 6:20–23; Mark 10:17–19; Luke 2:51–52; John 8:28–29; Ephesians 6:1–4; 1 Timothy 5:4.

Day 6
The Sixth to Ninth Commandments: people (6 and 7), possessions (8) and values (9): Exodus 20:13; Matthew 5:21–24; Exodus 20:14; Matthew 5:27–30; Exodus 20:15; Ephesians 4:28; Exodus 20:16; Ephesians 4:25, 29.

Day 7
The Tenth Commandment: guardianship of the heart:

Exodus 20:17; Ephesians 5:3–5; 1 Timothy 6:6–10; Hebrews 13:5–6.

Questions

1. Which commandment most convicts you at the moment? Take time to reflect and talk to God about it.
2. Does it surprise you that any of the commandments are part of God's top ten priorities for holy living? What does that tell you about God, and about yourself?

At home with the holy God

The first desire of our Redeemer God is that his redeemed people should obey him. Indeed, to keep his law was not a new bondage but a proof that the old bondage was over (Exodus 20:2). God's law, as we have just seen, is the life we were made for.

The Old Testament has many words describing the law:

► God's law is 'testimony' ('*ēdâ*, e.g. Psalm 119:2 NIV, 'statutes'). In his law, the Lord has 'borne witness' to himself and his requirements.

► This self-revelation of the Lord was given in 'law', as the word *tôrâ* is most frequently translated. Its true meaning, however, is 'teaching' (e.g. Psalm 119:1 NIV, 'law') – such teaching as a loving parent shares with a loved child (e.g. Proverbs 3:1; 6:20).

► This 'teaching' comes from God as a 'word' (*dābār*, e.g. Psalm 119:28) – that is, an intelligible body of truth, imparted verbally, to be pondered and applied.

► But the Lord's testimony is also imperishable: it is a 'statute' (*ḥōq*), a permanent enactment (e.g. Psalm 119:5 NIV, 'decrees'), like something engraved (verb *ḥāqaq*) on a rock, which cannot be erased and does not change with time.

► The word 'judgment' (*mišpāṭ*, e.g. Psalm 119:7 NIV, 'laws') describes an authoritative decision, such as a king or judge would make, settling an issue. See

1 Kings 3:28, where the NIV's 'verdict ... given' is, literally, 'judgment ... judged'.

▶ 'Precept' (*piqqûd*, e.g. Psalm 119:4) and 'command' (*miṣwâ*, e.g. Psalm 119:10) are pretty well synonymous. If a distinction can be drawn, 'command' stresses that God's law is given to be obeyed; 'precept' stresses the application of the law even to the smallest detail of life.

▶ Taken as a whole, God's law is a 'way' (*derek*, e.g. Psalm 119:3), a characteristic or distinct lifestyle, as when we say about someone, 'It's just his way!'

In the Old Testament, as in the New (e.g. Acts 5:32), obedience is a means of grace. A life based on the law of the Lord is under the blessing of God (Psalm 1:1), constantly nourished by secret springs and consistently fruitful (Psalm 1:2–3); and the way of obedience is the way of liberty (Psalm 119:45).

That's all very well, but ...

Into this attractive picture of living a truly human life through obedience to God's law, the horrible reality of sin intrudes. *Sinners do not, will not, and cannot* keep the law, however magnetic it may seem at times or however appealing its promise of the life that is life indeed. The Old Testament has three leading words for sin:

▶ The word usually translated 'sin' (*ḥaṭā'*) means to 'miss the mark'. In Judges 20:16 the verb is used of slingers hitting their target. In Psalm 51:2 David uses it in order to acknowledge that his misdemeanour with Bathsheba fell short of God's target, missed the mark of the good life. This word points to sin as a fact of our lives, whether through thought, word or deed.

▶ Then there is the word often translated 'iniquity'

('*āwôn*). It comes from a verb ('*āwâ*) meaning 'to bend or twist'; see the 'crooked' path in Lamentations 3:9 and the 'warped mind' of Proverbs 12:8. This word sees sin as rooted in a human nature that has become perverted from the Creator's intention, or, as we would say, a 'fallen' nature.

► The third word, often translated 'transgression', really means '(wilful) rebellion' (*peša'*), as, for example, of people rebelling against their lawful king (1 Kings 12:19). In relation to sin, it underlines the wilfulness of our sinful state. Over and over again we have bluntly and knowingly said 'no' to the law of God. 'We don't want this man to be our king' (Luke 19:14).

We are in a pretty hopeless state, then, when it comes to keeping God's law. In our occasional better moments we may seem to want it, but sin is a fact (we don't keep it), a condition of our fallen nature (we can't keep it), and a wilful rebellion (we won't keep it). On any and all of these grounds we have offended the God who gives us his law; we are alienated from him and he from us, and there can be no salvation till he is satisfied to have us back. There must not only be the change in us, called 'repentance'. There is an even deeper need that God should turn from judgment and wrath to favour and peace: his offended heart must be satisfied.

The God of the Passover

The oddest thing about the Passover (Exodus 12) is that the people actually did it! Just think: they were an immigrant people (Genesis 46:1–7; Exodus 1:1), viewed with loathing and fear by the Egyptians into whose land they had come (Exodus 1:9–12), and finally threatened with genocide (Exodus 1:22). To this people came the command, 'Take a lamb' (Exodus 12:3). Not only did it seem to have nothing to do with their actual needs, it also seemed pathetic and futile in such a setting. Yet they did it. It speaks much of Moses' leadership qualities. It speaks even more of an unmistakable, even overpowering, command from God.

And of course this is what it was. The Passover was the Lord's idea and provision, his way of doing things, the final move in his sole undertaking to bring his people from Egypt and to himself by liberation and redemption (Exodus 6:6–7). In what way, then, did the Passover 'redeem'?

The relevant part of Exodus 12, in which verses 43–51 really belong with chapter 13, falls into obvious divisions:

▶ verses 2–5, the choice of the lamb;

▶ verses 6–11, the killing and eating of the lamb;

▶ verses 12–13, the meaning of the Passover;

▶ verses 14–20, directions for the future, annual, week-long remembrance of the Passover;

▶ verses 21–28, directions for Passover night and for the future teaching of children;

▶ verses 29–30, the terrible events of the first Passover;

▶ verses 31–42, the exodus of Israel from Egypt.

It is a great story, marvellously told. Four truths are embedded in the story and they need to be underlined.

1 The choice of the lamb
The beast 'without defect' (Exodus 12:5, literally, 'perfect') was chosen so as to match the *number* (verse 4a) and *needs* (verse 4b) of those who would partake. Should there be any surplus meat, it must be destroyed by fire (verse 10), for the lamb has no other function than to match the number and needs of the people there and then, on that night of nights.

2 The change from the God of wrath to the God of peace

The keywords are, in Exodus 12:12, 'judgment'; and in verse 13, 'pass over … no destructive plague'. Once the Lord himself came into Egypt, everything took on a different 'shape'. The only thing that mattered now was how all the people in Egypt, Egyptians and Israelites alike, were related to him. Pharaoh's power and threats were no longer the issue. Only this mattered: how did they stand in relation to God? Sheltering under the blood of the lamb, all was peace. Judgment simply did not apply (cf. verses 22–23).

3 The Lord's redeemed pilgrims

Passover was an evening meal, a supper (Exodus 12:8), but they were to eat it, not in dressing-gowns and pyjamas, but in their day clothes, as those about to go on a journey, ready for action, and with a pilgrim staff in their hands (verse 11). Under the blood of the lamb, they were not only safe from the judgment of God (verses 13, 22–23), but Egypt and all that it meant was already a thing of the past. They had not yet left the land of bondage, but they were dressed for the journey. In principle and in reality they were already free to go on a pilgrimage. As soon as they entered the blood-marked houses, they were the Lord's redeemed people.

4 Why is the blood so powerful?

It was specifically the blood of the lamb that kept them safe from the judgment of God (Exodus 12:13, 22–23), and because they had taken shelter under the blood, they were already his liberated pilgrims (verse 11). This blood was, to put it mildly, wonder-working! First, the blood was, of course, a picture of death, of life terminated. And secondly, exactly whose blood was this? It was the blood of the chosen lamb, the lamb that was the exact equivalent of those who sheltered and ate, equivalent to their number and need.

Now, thirdly, look at it this way In every Egyptian

house one lay dead: the token but dreadful judgment of God, the death of the firstborn. In every Israelite house, too, one lay dead: the lamb, the equivalent, not just of the physically firstborn, but of the whole people whom God set out to redeem, the whole people whom he called his 'firstborn son' (Exodus 4:22), whose number and needs the lamb matched. The lamb died instead of the Lord's firstborn, the whole people it substituted for, all those who sheltered beneath its blood and ate its flesh. In the death of the substitute, God's judgment is satisfied, his people are saved and are already his liberated pilgrims.

End and beginning

We must now move on to Exodus 24:4–8, the ceremony at Mount Sinai in which the covenant with Israel was ratified.

1 A picture
The Lord had promised (Exodus 6:6–7) to bring his people to himself, and he did so (19:4). The resulting situation is now depicted by twelve pillars gathered round an altar (24:4). The symbols need no explanation. What God has done is, as we might say, set in concrete: the Lord, represented by the altar, and around him, in stone for permanency, his twelve tribes.

2 A reminder
They would have understood perfectly the link Moses made (Exodus 24:8) between 'covenant' and 'blood', because they had, just two months earlier (19:1), been through the Passover. By the blood, the substitutionary death of the lamb, they had been shielded from judgment, and the Lord had 'passed over' their houses. The blood of the lamb brought them into peace with God.

3 A promise
Moses 're-enacted' the double power of the blood: on the one hand, it allayed the wrath of God. Therefore, as his

first move, Moses sprinkled the altar: the blood has power Godward, satisfying God's righteous judgment. But, next, he read out God's law, and the people pledged obedience (Exodus 24:7). As soon as they did so, Moses sprinkled the rest of the blood over them (verse 8) In other words, as they set out on the life of obedience, they were still sheltered by the blood of the lamb (cf. 1 John 1:7). Those once under the blood are always under the blood. In their life of pilgrim obedience, with all its many hazards, faults and failings, the power of the blood remains available to keep them safe with a holy God.

The sacrifices

Blood – that is, the death of a substitute – had brought them into peace with God, and forever now blood will keep them in fellowship with him by means of the appointed offerings. This becomes very clear if we read straight through from the end of Exodus into the opening verses of Leviticus. Moses had just pitched the tabernacle for the first time. Everything had been done according to the Lord's specification (Exodus 40:16), the cloud of the Lord's presence covered the great tent, and the Lord in all his glory came to dwell among his people (verse 34). But though the Lord was 'at home', none, not even Moses, could enter his presence (verse 35). While Moses was facing this reality of exclusion, a Voice came from the tabernacle (Leviticus 1:1) which said (literally), 'When one of you brings near a "bringing near" to the Lord, it is from your livestock, herd or flock, that you must bring near your "bringing near"' (verse 2). To make an offering is to come 'near'; the offering is what 'brings near'. The presence of God is barred to sinners, but the appointed sacrifices bring us near to God.

The God-given sacrifices

This is the meaning of the sacrifices the Lord appointed through Moses: they implement and prolong what was achieved at the Passover: sinners can live in fellowship with the Holy One.

Three main sacrifices were commanded: the burnt offering, the peace offering and the sin offering.

The burnt offering (Leviticus 1)
The burnt offering expressed the double idea of acceptance before God and dedication to God (Leviticus 1:4). Its scent is sweet to the Lord (Leviticus 1:9; cf. Genesis 8:21–22), symbolizing both his pleasure in it and in the one who offers it. This truth of 'acceptance' is underlined when the burnt offering reappears as part of the peace offering: the fat of the offering (Leviticus 3:3ff.) is a burnt offering in miniature, and is called 'the bread of the offering' (Leviticus 3:11; cf. 21:8). The Lord, accepting the offering and the offerer, is delighted to sit at table, in fellowship with his people. But the burnt offering also expresses dedication. In Genesis 22:13 Abraham's burnt offering, in place of his son, showed that he was 'holding nothing back' (Genesis 22:12). This is the heart-searching level of devotion which constitutes true obedience.

The peace offering (Leviticus 3)
Also called the 'fellowship' offering, this looked both Godward and manward. Godward, it expressed thanksgiving and personal love (Leviticus 7:12, 16), but manward this joyous response to God's goodness had to be marked by fellowship with others. The priest had his share (Leviticus 7:31–34), but so had the family, the family retainers, resident aliens, and the needy (Deuteronomy 16:11). There was no such thing as vertical devotion Godward without horizontal caring and sharing.

The sin offering (Leviticus 4)
The object of the sin-offering was forgiveness and atonement (verses 20, 26, 31, 35). Awareness of a particular fault brought the individual sinner with his offering (verse 23), and by means of the offering divine forgiveness became a reality (verses 20, 26, 31, 35).

A key act

One action is common to all three classes of sacrifice: the offerer was required to lay his hand on the head of the offering (Leviticus 1:4; 3:2; 4:4). The meaning of this act becomes clear in the ritual of the Day of Atonement (Leviticus 16). On this day the Lord provided atonement for all the sins of his people in the past year. The High Priest was the officiant, and this is what he did. First, he took the blood of the sin offering right into the Holy of Holies, into the very presence of God (Leviticus 16:11–17), where he was allowed to go only once in the year (Hebrews 9:7, 11–12). This was the effective act of atonement, hidden from public gaze. But the Lord, in mercy, wanted his people to know what had happened, and to be fully assured that their sins were gone. Therefore he appointed a public ceremony. The High Priest took a second beast (Leviticus 16:20–22), and, laying his hand on its head, he recited over it all the iniquities, transgressions and sins (see above) of the people 'and put them on the goat's head' so that it became the sin-bearing goat (verse 22). Thus, symbolically, their sins were borne by another, and they saw them being carried away, never to be seen again.

The laying on of hands, therefore, is the way by which offerers identified the beast with their need. The hand became a sort of moral bridge by which sin crossed from sinners to their guiltless offering. Through the laying on of the hand, the offering was nominated as, and became a substitute for, the sinner, standing in his place, bearing his sin, discharging his debt and paying his penalty.

A key verse

All this is made clear in the one verse which defines what the sacrifices were all about: Leviticus 17:11. The verb translated 'to make atonement' is, in Hebrew, *kāpar*. In its simple form this means 'to cover', like Noah 'covered' the ark with pitch (Genesis 6:14 NIV, 'coat'). The intensive form of the verb, *kipper*, came to be used as a technical theological term, 'covering' sin, 'making atonement' Does this mean just hiding sin away out of sight, sweeping it under the carpet, as the wood of the ark disappeared under a coating of tar? No indeed. There is another meaning of 'covering' which we still use: the exact amount of money that covers a debt. This is what atonement means: the provision of that which covers our need, not by hiding it, but by dealing with it, settling the account so that the debt is actually gone, and no further claim can ever be made.

So Leviticus 17:11, translated literally, says:

> For the soul of the flesh is in the blood; And I have myself given it to you on the altar to pay the atonement price for your souls. For it is the blood that pays the atonement price in the place of the soul / at the expense of the soul.

Blood and flesh together mean life, but separate them, and death follows. The blood, the death of the sacrificial victim, is God's provision and gift, not a good idea of ours or a present given in order to put God under pressure or obligation to us. It is his idea and his gift of grace. The death of the beast pays the atonement price, both *taking the place of* our forfeited, sinful lives, and *at the expense of* its own, for, as indicated above, the final line of the verse (using the Hebrew preposition *bě*) can bear either meaning.

A real and present benefit

As the 'Israel' of God, we can look back, and, seeing everything in the light of Jesus, we can agree with Hebrews 10:4 that animal blood cannot take away sin. But our ancestors of the old covenant did not offer their sacrifices as a sort of expedient until the perfect sacrifice came along. The Lord gave them the sacrifices in order to convey actual spiritual benefits. Through them he promised atonement, and forgiveness (e.g. Leviticus 1:4; 4:20, 26; 17:11). In the Psalms we find Old Testament believers living in the reality of sins forgiven (e.g. Psalms 32:1–2; 51:11–13; 2 Samuel 12:13). Indeed, their enjoyment of spiritual blessings, their revelling in the knowledge and fellowship of God, is something we would envy and covet!

Nevertheless, we see Jesus in all this. He is God's final gift and his blood has paid the atonement price in *our* place and at *his* expense. Old Testament sacrifices proclaim New Testament truth, because the Bible is one book.

Passover week

The Passover sacrifice was offered *in Egypt* in order to bring the Lord's Israel *out of Egypt* and *to the Lord* (Exodus 6:6–7). It did exactly that (Exodus 14:13; 19:4). After that the Passover could not be offered again: the annual offering was a remembrance of what had happened 'once for all'. It is, therefore, a special preview of Calvary.

Spend Passover week with Exodus 12.

Day 1
The equivalent Lamb: Exodus 12:3–4; Isaiah 53:6; Romans 3:24–25; 1 Peter 2:24.

Day 2
The perfect Lamb: Exodus 12:5; Isaiah 53:9; 1 Peter 3:18.

Day 3
Responsibility for the death of the Lamb: Exodus 12:6; Isaiah 53:7–8; Acts 2:23.

Day 4
Taking shelter under the blood of the Lamb: Exodus 12:7; Isaiah 53:10 (NIV margin; NKJV); 1 Peter 1:18–21.

Day 5
The Lamb, our necessary food: Exodus 12:8; Isaiah 55:1–2; John 6:35, 53–57, 63.

Day 6
Passover and pilgrimage: Exodus 12:11; Philippians 2:12–15; Hebrews 10:19–25.

Day 7
The power of the blood of the Lamb: Exodus 12:12–13, 22–23; Romans 5:8–9; Colossians 1:20; Hebrews 9:12–14; Revelation 7:14–15.

Questions

1. What does the Old Testament sacrificial system tell you about Jesus' death on the cross?
2. Explore your response to his sacrifice and turn this into prayer and thanksgiving.

Great stories, one story

The Hebrew Bible is traditionally divided into three sections: *the Law* (Genesis to Deuteronomy); *the Prophets*, divided into the *Former Prophets* (Joshua, Judges, Samuel and Kings) and the *Latter Prophets* (Isaiah, Jeremiah, Ezekiel; Hosea to Malachi); and *the Writings* (Psalms, Proverbs, Job, Song of Songs, Ruth, Lamentations, Ecclesiastes, Esther, Daniel, Ezra, Nehemiah, Chronicles). The order of the books in our English Bibles came through the Greek translation of the Old Testament, known as the Septuagint (or the LXX).

The Hebrew order is actually more sensible, and probably reflects the way the canon, or the authoritative collection of books, came together But, we may wonder, why are some history books called 'the *Former Prophets*'? They are former, of course, because they precede the latter prophets in the collection, but why is *history* called *prophecy*?

All history writing is a selection made from everything that could be written down, and all authors who write history select what they feel to be important for posterity. Selection has to be made, for even if a writer could know and write down everything that happened, a book that size would be hard pressed to find a publisher! Many historians see no plan or purpose in the way history 'works out', yet even they must sift out what they want to put on paper – in other words, what they think 'important' from all the facts available to them. They have to make a selection. John (21:25) says his Gospel was selectively written.

The same is true of Matthew, Mark and Luke, and, indeed, of all Bible history. None of the histories tells us all we would like to know, only what we need to know, and only what the authors, under the Holy Spirit, decided we ought to know. The Gospel writers said, in effect, 'These are the facts you need in order to know Jesus.' And in the same way, the Old Testament historians selected their information so that we would know how the Lord rules in history, orders it so as to achieve his purposes – in a word, reveals himself through what he does. This does not, of course, mean that any facts were made up or falsified or twisted out of shape in order to make them tell God's story. The Lord was revealed along the grain of events as they happened. History is itself a revelation of God, his story. This is why Bible history is 'prophecy'.

Joshua, the bridging man and his bridging book

Joshua was Moses' personal assistant (Exodus 24:13; 33:11; Numbers 1:28; Deuteronomy 1:38; etc.) and chosen successor (Deuteronomy 31:7). Even though we first meet him as a field commander (Exodus 17:8–9), he was an unlikely choice for a military career. For surely only a naturally timid, hesitant, even indecisive person would need so many urgings, and from different people too, to be strong, courageous and unafraid (Deuteronomy 31:6–8, 23; Joshua 1:6–7, 9, 18). Yet that was Joshua's work in the Lord's plan: the timid assistant taking over from the towering figure of Moses to lead the people over Jordan and into the battle for their inheritance. His book is the account of his stewardship. For simplicity, we can see the book of Joshua in five sections:

1. Joshua takes up his leadership (1:1–9).
2. Crossing into Canaan, beginning to possess (1:10 – 5:12).
3. Joshua's wars of conquest (5:13 – 12:24).
    a. The central powers (5:13 – 8:29).
    b. The southern coalition (9:1 – 10:43).

    c. The northern alliance (11:1–15).
    d. Summary: Joshua's victories (11:16 – 12:3).
  4. The allocation of the land (13:1 – 22:34).
  5. Joshua's farewell and death (23:1 – 24:33).

Like all history writing in the Bible, the book of Joshua is a great story, brilliantly told, and in the first instance to be read as such. But if Bible history is prophecy, we have to ask a deeper question: what is its testimony about the Lord? What is its abiding message to the Lord's people then and now?

Within the history of how the Promised Land was possessed, there are two interlocking themes:

▶ The presence of the Lord with his people as the promise-keeping God (e.g. Joshua 1:3–5, 9; 2:9–11; 3:7; 6:17; 10:8, 11, 25, 42; 11:6, 23; 21:43–45; 22:4; 23:14).

▶ Obeying the Word of the Lord as the key factor in the life of the Lord's people (e.g. Joshua 1:7–8, 13; 4:8, 10; 5:13–15; 7:10–12; 8:27; 10:40; 11:15; 14:5; 22:2; 23:6, 8–13).

Joshua 1:7–8 commends 'this book of the Law' to Joshua himself as the recipe for successful living, and at the end (23:6) Joshua uses identical words to call his people to fashion their life in obedience to God's truth. As soon, then, as Joshua got a foothold in Canaan (5:1–9), he dared to obey a command to circumcise his fighting men, an operation which would immediately immobilize them (cf. Genesis 34:25). Nothing is more important for the Lord's people than to know themselves as those to whom the covenant promises have been made, and to bring themselves within the orbit of covenant obedience. In the same spirit, when he achieved his first victories in central Palestine, even though to the south and north lay powerful and as yet unsubdued foes, Joshua obeyed the command to identify Mounts Ebal and Gerizim with the curses and blessings of the covenant (Joshua 8:30–34; cf.

Deuteronomy 27:11–13). In other words, first things first! The very land they live in is identified with the call to obey and the warning not to disobey, the way of life and the way of death, the life-giving Word and the dire consequence of neglecting it.

Joshua's own leadership was subject to exactly the same constraints. Devotion to the Word of God was the key to successful leadership (Joshua 1:7–8), and over and over the pattern is repeated that 'the Lord said … and Joshua said …' (e.g. 1:2, 11; 4:2, 4; 5:2–3; etc.). Significantly, therefore, Joshua's only defeat in battle (7:5) was due to disobedience (7:10–13), and his only failure in leadership, his mistaken treaty with the Gibeonites (9:1–27), was due to the fact that they 'sampled their provisions but did not enquire of the Lord' (9:14), an error in which Joshua himself was sadly complicit.

The book of Joshua is therefore an historical bridge, from the time of Moses in Egypt and the wilderness to life in Canaan under the Judges and later the Kings. It is also a theological and moral bridge, perpetuating the central place of the Word of God, the call to obey, and the requirement to live on earth by a supernatural code: to be the people wedded to the Word of the Lord.

Judges

It is always a good question to ask why a Bible book was written, for we must remember that individual books (like Judges) were not written because otherwise there would be a gap in the Bible! They were written, as books still are, because the author had something he wanted to say, some particular truth or insight. Whoever wrote Judges did indeed fill in some gaps. Where, for example, Joshua gives broad-brush treatment to the overall conquest of the Promised Land, Judges fills in some details of the way that individual tribes entered into their inheritance (Judges 1:1 – 2:7). Verses like Joshua 15:63; 16:10 expose failure to drive out the original inhabitants, and Judges records the subsequent suffering inflicted by those who ought to have been conquered (e.g. Judges 4:2). None of this, however, answers the question as to why Judges was written. For it too is 'prophecy', and we need to know what truth it sets out to share.

The book of Judges lives in our memories because of the scintillating individuals it portrays: the 'judges' and their deeds of derring-do. Who could forget the serene Deborah (Judges 4 – 5) and her sidekick Barak? Or little Gideon and his 300 men (6 – 8)? Or Jephthah with the colossal chip on his shoulder (11)? Or that archetypal buffoon, Samson (13 – 16), who could never resist either a joke or a girl? But for all their striking successes, the judges were all ultimately failures, bringing only limited respite from foreign domination: the eighty years of 3:30; the forty years of 5:31; 8:28; Jephthah's six years (12:7) and Samson's twenty years (16:31). But, in every case, as soon as the judge died, people went back to the old sinful ways that had got them into trouble in the first place (e.g. 8:33).

The problem was always 'sin', or as Judges 6:1 puts it, 'doing evil in the eyes of the Lord', which the same passage defines as, 'you have not listened to me' (verse 10). Responding to their evil, the Lord sent, not a military deliverer to deal with Midian, but a prophet (verse 7) to recall them to his Word, to bring them back to (literally) 'hearing him'. This is always the cardinal sin of the Lord's people: to sit loose to his Word, to stop hearing. Likewise, the sovereign remedy is to return to the Word of the Lord.

But were there particular evils besetting the people? It is the function of Judges 17 – 21 to answer this question, and the chapters bring us down from the dizzy heights of the gifted leaders to the grass-roots level of ordinary folk. They expose four areas of wrongdoing: religious apostasy (17:1–13), social violence (18:1–31), sexual immorality (19:1–30) and national breakdown (20:1 – 21:25). It is a dark picture, and the passage from Judges 1 – 16 into 17 – 21 is like leaving the intermittent sunshine and entering a black, damp cellar.

The gloom, however, is relieved by a confidently proposed solution. Four times, once for each area of wrongdoing, the author diagnoses a cause and implies a remedy:

▶ 'In those days Israel had no king; everyone did as he saw fit' (17:6).

▶ 'In those days Israel had no king' (18:1).

▶ 'In those days Israel had no king' (19:1).

▶ 'In those days Israel had no king; everyone did as he saw fit' (21:25).

The message is unmistakable: where there is no king, all these evidences of refusal of the Word of God are inevitable, but if only we had a king ...

Samuel and Kings

The books of Samuel and Kings continue the standard of history-writing achieved in Joshua and Judges: brilliant storytelling and great characters. But the narrative is purposeful: it is a search for the king who will prove to be the solution for all ills.

The books of Samuel get their title from the fact that the first twelve chapters centre for the most part on Samuel, the last of the Judges (1 Samuel 12:10–11) and Israel's 'kingmaker' (1 Samuel 8 – 12).

The choice of king first fell on Saul (1 Samuel 9 – 10), a man of striking presence (9:2), good popular rating (11:15), the capacity to attract and retain loyalty (10:26), an irenic disposition (10:27; 11:12–13), and many of the military qualities demanded at the time (11:1–11). Saul is one of the most attractive men of the Bible, and not for nothing has he been referred to as 'the beloved Captain', but he was beset by personal insecurity (e.g. 10:20–22), which became chronic (18:6–9) and finally manic (18:11; 19:10; 20:31–33). Yet it was not Saul's insecurity, nor his incipient paranoia that lost him the throne, it was his disobedience. First, told by Samuel to wait seven days at Gilgal (10:8), he lost patience (13:7–10), and lost the opportunity to found a dynasty (13:13). Secondly, sent to execute the Lord's judgment on the Amalekites (15:2–3; cf. Exodus 17:8; Deuteronomy 25:17–19), he did not do so (1 Samuel 15:9), and was rejected personally from being king (15:23). Saul passed the Judges 17 test by cleansing the land of religious apostates, at least to the extent that 1 Samuel 28:3 records, but he presided over a violent (e.g. 22:17–19) and divided society (e.g. 23:21–28).

Saul, then, was not the ideal king whom the author of Judges saw as the solution for all ills. But neither was David, golden boy though he was, and the standard by which all subsequent kings were judged (e.g. 2 Kings 16:2; 18:3). He was a great king, by turns lovable (e.g. 2 Samuel 9) and exasperating (e.g. 2 Samuel 14:23–24), resolute in living within the Lord's will (e.g. 1 Samuel 26:8–10), stubborn in demanding his own way (e.g. 2 Samuel 24:2–4). Taking all with all, he was a worthy standard for his successors, but he was the king whose heart was right and whose heart was wrong. There, in a nutshell, is David! 'Great David' indeed, but was he the ideal king whom the book of Judges envisaged?

David's life of snakes and ladders

The story of David's life is told like this: start from the bottom left of the diagram and climb the 'ladder'; move to the top right and slide down the 'snake'.

Bathsheba (2 Sam. 11 – 12)
King of Israel (2 Sam. 5:1–5) — Amnon & Tamar (2 Sam. 13)
King of Judah (2 Sam. 2:4) — Absalom (2 Sam. 14 – 18)
Total loss (1 Sam. 30:1–6) — David's return (2 Sam. 119)
Rejection (1 Sam. 19 – 27) — Sheba's rebellion (2 Sam. 20)
Royal marriage (1 Sam. 18:17ff.) — Gibeonite fiasco (2 Sam. 21)
Acclaim (1 Sam. 18:1ff.) — The census (2 Sam. 24)
Goliath (1 Sam. 17) — David's decay (1 Kings 1)
David's anointing (1 Sam. 16) — David's will (1 Kings 2:1–10)

Some of these items, up and down, match each other significantly. David's accession as king balances against the collapse of his own family with Amnon and Absalom; his victory over Goliath is in contrast to his tragic decay in 1 Kings 1 where David, now a toothless tiger, is manipulated by internal palace cliques. Best king though he was, he was far from the best of all kings.

The most striking feature, however, of David's history is not found in this incident or that, but in the trajectory of the whole story. From the time of the secret anointing, even though David's pathway seems to us tortuous and unexpected (his life as a fugitive [1 Samuel 19:10] and an exile [27:1]), we sense that everything is quietly maturing towards his eventual kingship, as indeed it was. But after his double sin of adultery with Bathsheba and complicity in the virtual murder of her husband Uriah, the whole fabric of his life, family and rule steadily unravels, and the man who could so easily win friends (e.g. 1 Samuel 18:1) leaves a loathsome legacy of vindictiveness (1 Kings 2:5–9). To be sure, the Lord fully and graciously forgave his sin as soon as he repented (2 Samuel 12:13; cf. Psalm 51:1–3), but the episode had immediate consequences (2 Samuel 12:14), and even wider consequences that rippled on and on. David failed the third test of kingship in the Judges list: for all his great qualities he lacked the moral majesty needed to be the Messiah: 'Great David's Greater Son' was yet to come!

Solomon: the tests of wisdom

Of all the kings, Solomon was the one who had success handed to him on a plate! Aside from other things, David bequeathed a united kingdom. He had done the fighting, and Solomon could be what his name said he was, the 'man of peace'. Furthermore, passages like 1 Chronicles 29:1–9 suggest that the country was wealthy beyond anything previously known. We might say, Solomon had it made. He brought in new administrative procedures (1 Kings 4:7–19) which might ultimately have eroded the north/south tensions which had existed even in David's day, and which Absalom had exploited (2 Samuel 15:1–6). His boundaries were the most extended ever (1 Kings 4:21–24), with consequent revenue wealth (cf. 10:14–25). His people were prosperous and contented (4:25; 10:27). He had a strong regular army (4:26; 10:26). He possessed boundless wisdom and understanding (4:29–34). Rather than ask, 'So what went wrong?', we might well ask, 'What *could* go wrong?'

The answer is that there is no such thing as untested wisdom. The divine providence which was delighted to give Solomon the wisdom he requested (1 Kings 3:4–12), gave him also the things he did not ask for, but which would test him in the use of his God-given wisdom: would he hold to the way of wisdom under the pressure of unlimited wealth, and the plaudits of people (1 Kings 3:13), and the passage of time (3:14)? Marrying Pharaoh's daughter (3:1) was not a promising start – much good it did him (11:14, 19–21, 40)! – but it was only the beginning of Solomon's marital and sexual adventures (11:1–3). Grimly, with love came apostasy (11:4), so that the supreme temple-builder became, as an older man, the temple-corruptor (11:5–8). The Bible, for sure, doesn't believe in whitewash! The first of the Judges' tests (see Judges 17), religious defection, was Solomon's death knell.

The swinging spotlight

Solomon, who had the best chance, was also the last chance, for he left his kingdom to a nincompoop called Rehoboam (1 Kings 12), under whose mismanagement the kingdom of David divided into two and remained thus until both Israel (2 Kings 17, 722 BC) and Judah (2 Kings 25, 586 BC) came to an end, respectively at the hands of the superpowers of Assyria and Babylon.

But the hunt continued for the messianic king who would be the answer to all our problems. The books of Kings look like this:

The disappointed hope: David.
1 Kings 1:1 – 2:12
⇩

The flawed beginning (of David's line).
1 Kings 2:13 – 11:43
⇩

The swinging spotlight.
1 Kings 12:1 – 2 Kings 24:16
⇩

The inevitable end (of David's line).
2 Kings 24:17 – 25:26
⇩

The tiny spark of hope.
2 Kings 25:27–30

Every bit of this is important, and, of course, the stories in themselves are fascinating, but the major impression made by the books of Kings is, 'What an extraordinary way this is to write history!' At one moment we are in the southern kingdom of Judah, now north in Israel. King follows king with mind-baffling speed. Manasseh, who reigned fifty-five years, gets seventeen verses and only one fact recorded (2 Kings 21). And what a motley crew they are: good-hearted lads not up to the job, like Hezekiah (2 Kings 18 – 20); meddlers like Jehoshaphat with his incredibly foolish alliances (1 Kings 22; 2 Chronicles 19 – 20); the drivingly ambitious Jeroboams (1 Kings 11 – 14; 2 Kings 14); great disappointments like David and Solomon; occasional bright spots like Josiah (2 Kings 22 – 23); twenty-four-carat bad hats like Manasseh (2 Kings 21); and downright incompetents like Rehoboam at the start and Zedekiah at the end (1 Kings 12; 14; 2 Kings 24 – 25).

Fascinating history indeed, but why the swinging spotlight? Why not tell Judah's history and then Israel's, or vice versa? Why tangle the two together? Because the prophetic message of this history is what matters, and it can best be proclaimed by keeping the two kingdoms in parallel focus. Two sorts of kingship were in fact involved.

In the northern kingdom of Israel, men came to the throne for the most part by their individual talents, ambitions, and strong natural gifts of leadership. In its 200 years there were seven assassinations and one military coup. Of the nineteen kings who reigned, only eleven passed the crown to a son. Down south in Judah, succession was by inheritance, father to son, in the orderly line of David – a neat, organized system But neither monarchy produced the Messiah. Each failed one, or another, or all of the tests proposed in Judges. The perfect king, the answer to all our needs, is something that neither human talent nor succession even from David can achieve. Something more, Someone more, is required.

Chronicles: not an optional extra

And that something, or Someone, will certainly come. There is no doubt about that! The Lord God does not renege on his promises, give up on his people, or adjust his purposes.

This is what the two books of Chronicles are all about. Even though they cover much the same ground as Kings, they do so with compelling vividness and excitement, with much new information drawn from different sources, with old facts given new perspectives. Above all they respond to the great 'hunt for the Messiah' with a resounding 'yes', an affirmation of God, and his reliability, his trustworthiness and the infallible accomplishment of what he has planned.

It would be a daring author nowadays – or one with a death wish – who opened his book with nine chapters of names! Nothing exciting about that, you might well say. Quite the reverse – a turn-off if ever there was one. Of course, the lists are not exciting reading, but the implication they convey, the reason for their presence, is exciting, if only we can catch the vision. The first word of Chronicles is 'Adam', a shorthand way of saying that we are meeting with the work of God at its most universal. The huge number of absolute unknowns in the subsequent lists points to the fact that this great, ceaseless Divine Worker never loses sight of the ongoing march of his purposes. The unworthy, the recalcitrant, the positively horrid, all are caught up, sovereignly, into an irresistible river in spate, stemming from God, just as strong if it seems to flow underground or into the sand. The last word of Chronicles is that Cyrus the Persian, wretched imperialist that he was, would-be monarch of all he surveyed, the most powerful man in the world, is, when it comes down to it, but a tool to promote the plan of the God of Israel (cf. Proverbs 21:1).

It is at this point that Chronicles itself ends, and also brings the Old Testament (of which it is the last in the Hebrew arrangement of the books) to an end. The purpose of God has not run into the sand after all. God is still on the throne, and the world is still in his hands, just as much as when Adam was created. The line of David, now incognito, lives on, and some glad day, one who might otherwise have worn the crown, a local builder in Nazareth, an incomparable man named Joseph, will acknowledge as if his own the son of his fiancée, Mary, and the long-awaited triumph will have come.

When Chronicles finishes its lists of names, it becomes almost exclusively a book focusing on David and his successors, the royal city of Jerusalem and its temple. The occasional flashes of goodness and righteousness that shone in David's heirs and successors serve only to illuminate the dire failure of any of them to fulfil the messianic hope. Rather, Chronicles, that most charitable of books about Judahite royalty, keeps an unflinching eye on the wickedness of kings, priests and people, and on the inescapable sequence of sin and punishment, disobedience and calamity that is the hallmark of a world in the hands of the Holy God. But judgment never had the last word; calamity was never the end. Chronicles was written for the post-exilic people. Their memory included the devastation of David's kingdom by the Babylonians, the firing of the temple, the sack of the city, the carrying off of the people into exile. It was all very well for Isaiah to paint a picture of a returning people almost literally trailing clouds of glory, but the return of the exiles, allowed by Cyrus, was by comparison a miserable affair, a tiny company coming back to a ruined country and a life of grinding endeavour and local opposition, still under alien rule, with no kingdom, no king, no David! How important that they hear the message that not even failure, or opposition, or sin, or disobedience can turn the Lord aside. He is not a mere man that he should play false, nor a mere human that he should be untruthful. He has spoken and he will do it. He has commanded blessing and his people will yet be blessed (cf. Numbers 23:1–20).

What a message for a dark day! And it is part of the imperishable Word of God, and as true for us as it was when it was first written.

Ezra/Nehemiah: facing the long night of hope

After Ezra 1 – 5 has summarized the story of the returned community, following Cyrus' edict, Ezra 6 – Nehemiah 13 tells the story of two men. It is possible that these books were written down by the same anonymous author who gave us Chronicles. The suitability of the three books to each other is striking. If Chronicles is keen for us to learn that, although disobedience attracts due calamity, mercy and the triumph of God have the last word, the memoir of Ezra and Nehemiah balances the picture by recording the wonders that even one obedient man can perform under God. If Chronicles warns us away from disobedience, Ezra and Nehemiah woo us into the obedient life. Ezra comes on the scene as the man who knows the Word of God (Ezra 7:6, 10, 14, 25), and is commissioned to bring his people under God's teaching. Nehemiah, the courtier-butler (Nehemiah 1:11b) turned builder (Nehemiah 2:5), aided by Ezra, actually brings the people of his brand-new city under the Word of God (Nehemiah 8:1–12), and furnishes us with our last picture of God's people as the night of hope closes in on them, a people attentive to his Word (Nehemiah 8:13–18). When that night draws to an end, the

Messiah will come and day will break (Luke 1:78–79), but till then their ideal posture is to hear attentively what the Lord has written in his book.

Ruth: a case in point

In the English Bible, Ruth follows Judges, and there is a good logic to that. The story it tells belongs (Ruth 1:1) in the days when the Judges judged, and serves to show that the sour darkness of Judges 17 – 21 was by no means the whole truth about the people of God. There were those who continued to love the name of the Lord. The frightening sense of the Lord's withdrawal from the scene which dominates the last chapters of Judges needs to be balanced by this story of his presence and tender care of individuals, and by its picture of godly and spiritual community life (e.g. Ruth 2:4). But in the Hebrew Bible, Ruth is in the final division of the canon, suggesting that, whenever this delightful sidelight on David's story (cf. 4:13–22) was actually recorded, its popular appeal flowered for the post-exilic people. Rightly so! Did they cry out, like Naomi, 'the Almighty has dealt very bitterly with me' (1:20)? Then let them learn that, just as for Naomi, it would be true for them that 'the Lord brought me home' (1:21). Did they long for the return of David, predicted by Ezekiel (34:23–24)? Then let them consider that long ago, this unknown woman and her obscure family, including her 'foreign' daughter-in-law, were carriers of the 'messianic virus', all unknowingly, and through them, in God's time, Ruth bore Obed to Boaz, Obed was the father of Jesse, and Jesse was the father of David (Ruth 4:17–22).

Is Ruth just a happy love-story? It is all of that, the 'Mills and Boon' of the Old Testament! But it is much, much more. Like all biblical history, it is prophecy, a proclamation of the faithful, tender, unfailing God and his promises, a God under whose wings (Ruth 2:12) there is shelter and security.

The kings in seven soundbites

Day 1
The first king was Saul (c. 1040 BC). 1 Samuel 12:11–12 hints that depending on the Lord to raise up leaders as needs arose was too great a strain on the people's faith. They wanted the security of a permanent institution. Saul was great, bringing security (14:47–48), but he failed in obedience (13:1–14; 15:17–26).

Day 2
David (c. 1000 BC) loved the Lord, but he loved Bathsheba too! He was the Lord's anointed (1 Samuel 16:1–13), the people's choice (2 Samuel 2:1–4; 5:1–5). The Lord promised him an endless line (2 Samuel 7:15–16). But came the day when (perhaps) he couldn't help seeing but he could help looking (2 Samuel 11:1–2).

Day 3
Solomon (c. 960 BC), the all-wise (1 Kings 3:4–14) who became the old fool (1 Kings 11:1–8).

Day 4
Rehoboam (c. 920 BC) who threw it all away (1 Kings 12:1–16), and Jeroboam who could have made it (11:29–38) but didn't (12:25–33).

Day 5
Occasional brighter times like that of Hezekiah (c. 716 BC, 2 Kings 18:1–6) or Josiah (c. 640 BC, 2 Kings 22:1–10).

Day 6
Mostly inadequates like Zedekiah (c. 590 BC, 2 Kings 24:17 – 25:7), the last Davidic king to reign until the One came whose reign is forever (Luke 1:32).

Day 7
Although no further kings reigned in Jerusalem, the line

did not die out (2 Kings 25:27–30). Though humans fail, the Lord's purposes and promises continue.

Questions

1. What qualities do you admire in a leader? How do these compare with the qualities shown in the Old Testament kings?
2. Identify any areas of your life where you are in a position of leadership – whether formal or informal. Which of the qualities of the Old Testament kings would you like to imitate, or avoid?
3. What do the tales of motley kings tell us about our God? How does God use flawed people today to fulfil his purposes?

What hymn book do you use?

Singing came naturally to Old Testament believers. 'Then Moses ... sang' (Exodus 15:1) when they had marched through the Red Sea and were at last safely out of Egypt's clutches. Miriam and her band of women spontaneously joined in 'with tambourines and dancing' (Exodus 15:20). Deborah and Barak sang 'on that day' (Judges 5:1) when Sisera was routed and lay dead. 'Hannah prayed', says 1 Samuel 2:1, but her prayer sounded like a song. Maybe she and Elkanah, on their way to Samuel's dedication, spent time picking a hymn for the service! Did Hannah say: 'Do let's have "My heart rejoices in the Lord"'? If she did, she said something of which all the singers would have approved: their songs were not about themselves, but about the Lord, his greatness and goodness, his kindly and marvellous works. They were responding, by singing, to what he is and had done. Likewise, Isaiah foretold the coming song of salvation (Isaiah 12:1–6) and foresaw redeemed Zion exploding into song (54:1), and overheard the singing pilgrims on their way home (24:13–16; cf. 25:1; 26:1) to their strong city. Isaiah 24 – 27 is indeed best read as a 'Pilgrims' Cantata'. Lots of other passages from the prophets too are encouragements to sing, and probably are themselves songs (e.g. Zephaniah 3:14–17).

The great collection

It was singing all the way in the Old Testament, and the book we call the Psalms is the concentrated expression of that great tradition of spiritual celebration. The Psalms, of course, reflect all aspects of life, but their prevailing mood is the greatness and goodness of God (e.g. 18:1–3; 59:16–17), and the praise which is his due (e.g. 145). The recurring summons to 'sing to the Lord a new song' (98:1; cf. 33:3; 40:3; 96:1; 144:9; 149:1) underlines the fact of *responsive* singing: he has acted and his fresh acts merit fresh praise; he has done it all and nothing is left for us to do but to rejoice and sing. Indeed, in the Bible, singing has this special significance: it is our reponse to God's saving acts in which we have had no part, and to which we have made no contribution: it is our joyful acknowledgment that in our helplessness the Lord has done everything. 'Song' is a motif, expressing the truth that salvation is all of God, and our only part is to sing over what has been done for us.

Gathering the collection

Is it any wonder, then, that Psalms is the largest book in the whole Bible? The Lord's praises are inexhaustible; the Lord's people are a singing people.

We know very little about how the book of Psalms was actually assembled. Out of 150 psalms, 110 have introductory titles or headings. In the Hebrew Bible these are reckoned as part of the text itself, and should be treated with equal seriousness, even though much of the information is now obscure.

Fifty-two psalms are described as *mizmôr* (e.g. 3 – 5) or 'psalm' (NIV). Coming from the verb *zāmar*, 'to make music', *mizmôr* may mean 'suitable/set for singing'. Next most frequent is the word *šîr*, 'a song' (fourteen times, e.g. 30; 46). How does this differ from *mizmôr*? Some difference was intended, because Psalm 108 has both words.

The use of accompanying 'strings' is noted in Psalms 4; 6 etc., and 'flutes' are noted in Psalm 5 The NIV, probably correctly, adds the explanatory words, 'set to the tune' in Psalms 9; 22; 45; 56; 57 – 60; 69; 80. Unexplained (but probably musical) terms occur in Psalms 16 (*miktām*, with five other psalms); 8 (*gittît*, with two others); 6 (*šĕmînît*); 7 (*šiggāyôn*); 88 (*mahǎlat lĕʿannôt*, but see NIV margin); 53 (*mahalath*) Equally unexplained is the word *selah* which occurs nearly seventy-five times, and comes within the psalms in question (e.g. 3:2, 4, 8), presumably directing how the psalm was used in worship. Maybe it was a musical interlude or a pause for meditation, but nothing is known for certain.

Psalms 17; 86; 90 are singled out as prayers (cf. 102), Psalm 100 for giving thanks, Psalm 92 for the Sabbath, Psalm 60 for teaching. Since these descriptions could seemingly just as easily apply to so many other psalms, we must assume that this rubric was somehow appropriate for the psalm when it was first composed.

Smaller collections

The book of Psalms seems to incorporate small, and, probably, originally separate, collections. One such would have been the 'songs of ascents' (Psalms 120 – 134), best thought of as a pilgrims' hymn book for use by travelling companies going up to Jerusalem. But Psalms 93 – 100 could have been royal praise, celebrating the Lord's kingship over Israel and the world. Maybe there was an annual festival of kingship, like our Ascension Day, for which this small hymn book was first gathered. Likewise, Psalms 113 – 118 and 146 – 150 are sustained outbursts of praise. Understandably, such songbooks could not be allowed to disappear, and so were brought, *in toto*, into the final collection.

Nearly seventy psalms are described as (literally) 'to David', including almost every psalm in 3 – 70, and again sixteen psalms in 101 – 144. 'To David' does not necessarily mean authorship. It could mean 'ascribed to' or 'dedicated to' or 'belonging to' (i.e. a collection that David made), but the Bible's strong association of David with spiritual composition (e.g. 2 Samuel 22:1; 23:1) supports the translation 'by David', and the psalms in question suit David's time and authorship. Their occurrence in two blocks, however, suggests that they are earlier collections, given their final home in the Psalms. Asaph (cf. 1 Chronicles 15:16–17; 16:4–6) and the sons of Korah (6:22) have respectively twelve and eleven outstandingly beautiful psalms (e.g. Psalms 81 – 83; 44 – 49). We may presume that these were temple choirs, and the psalms were culled from their repertoire.

And finally ...

All through the years of the Davidic monarchy in Jerusalem, the temple, with its constant round of services, and its importance as the goal of pilgrimage, would have stimulated the production and collection of worship songs. Events of national and spiritual significance like the death of David, or the reconstitution of the temple under Joash (2 Kings 12) or Josiah (2 Kings 22), would have prompted the production of hymn books, in the same way that notable religious occasions do so today. In 586 BC, the temple of Solomon (1 Kings 5 – 8) was destroyed (2 Kings 25:9), and remained in ruins until the people returned from Babylon in 539 BC. The abortive start then made (Ezra 1 – 3) resulted in the second temple, completed in 516 BC (Ezra 5 – 6; Haggai). It is reasonable to assume that part of the preparation for the restored temple would have been a serious attempt to produce a definitive book of worship, and it was probably at this time that what we call 'the Psalms' achieved its present form. In any case, there is no need to date any psalm later than the date that Psalm 137 suggests for itself – that is, the early days of the return from Babylon when the miseries of exile were still freshly remembered.

One last puzzle remains: why did the final compilers divide the collection into five parts: Psalms 1 – 41; 42 – 72; 73 – 89; 90 – 106; 107 – 150? To this and many other questions we have no answer, but we can shout our thanks back over the centuries to those devoted people who, under God, whether as writers, conservators or editors, gave us this incomparable anthology of prayer, praise and spiritual meditation and direction.

David in autobiographical mode

Among the Psalms ascribed to David are fourteen which owe their headings to incidents in David's life: 3; 7; 18; 30; 34; 51; 52; 54; 56; 57; 59; 60; 63; 142.

Psalm 7

This refers to Cush the Benjamite, a character not otherwise known. We do know that the Benjamite King Saul (1 Samuel 9:1–2) surrounded himself with fellow Benjamites (22:7), and that he was incited against David by slandering tongues (24:9; 26:19). This psalm relates to a time when words could really damage David; possibly, therefore, it dates from the early days of the Saul–David saga (see 18:10–25).

Psalm 18

Psalm 18 concludes the same period. David looks back and recalls the almighty power of God on his side. We can, however, read the whole story in 1 Samuel without finding any reference to earthquake (verse 7), devouring fire (verse 8), clouds, hailstones, or fire (verse 12), thunder and lightning (verses 12–14). So what is David saying? A most important lesson about the Psalms arises here: the Hebrews did not write narrative poetry in the sense of putting an historical record into poetic form. As with all Bible history writing, it was what the facts meant that mattered (cf. Psalms 78; 105 – 106). So, in the body of Psalm 7 the 'Cush' in the heading is not mentioned again, for it is not Cush's part in the incident that really matters, but rather the meaning of the event – the savage and malignant power of the tongue, the efficacy of prayer, the offence given to the Lord, and the principle of retribution built into the very nature of things. Likewise, in Psalm 18, as David pondered his past, he saw that only the Lord, working in his almightiness, with every resource at his disposal, could have brought him through. He uses the 'forces of nature' *illustratively, not descriptively*. They are a motif, a way of affirming that the Lord was acting in power.

Psalm 34

This is a most interesting example of the autobiographical David, because its heading seems to be at loggerheads with the facts in 1 Samuel 21:10–15. David ran for his life, and found a (hopefully) anonymous refuge at the court of Achish, king of Gath (called by his throne-name, Abimelech, in the psalm heading; cf. Genesis 26:1). But once David was recognized, Achish realized he had a valuable hostage in his hands, and David found himself in danger of being used as a pawn in some diplomatic deal with Saul. He had to get away. But how? Pretend to be mad! So he began to exhibit personal habits suggesting that he was not in his right mind, and went round scribbling graffiti. Achish had soon had enough, and David was allowed to make his escape. What a story – and with a great ring of truth! David could well pride himself on his resourcefulness.

But when he came to write up the incident, why, he realized it wasn't like that at all. The 'real story' lay behind the surface story. He had prayed about it, hadn't he (Psalm 34:4, 6)? And suddenly he knew for certain that his deliverance was not due to his own clever cunning but to the intervention of the good God (verse 8) who hears prayer and is near those who call upon him (verses 17–18).

In recording this mediation on a time of extreme danger, and putting the record straight, David used an alphabetic form which appears elsewhere in the Psalms, with each verse beginning with the letters of the Hebrew alphabet taken in turn. This is not just a clever or artificial literary exercise. We say 'A to Z' to stress completeness. In Psalm 34, we have an 'A to Z for a time of trouble'. Other 'A to Z' psalms are, for example, Psalm 25, with the same theme as Psalm 34; Psalm 37, an A-B-C for personal spiritual conflict; and, of course, the mighty Psalm 119, the golden A-B-C of the Word of God, where each letter gets eight verses to itself. Sometimes the alphabetic acrostic is incomplete or 'broken', maybe because the theme cannot be totally expressed (as in the Hebrew text of Psalm 145, an A-B-C of the glory of God), or to reflect the brokenness of life in a time of stress (as Psalms 9 – 10).

Psalm 51

This is probably the most famous of the 'autobiographical' psalms – though many commentators, surprisingly, have questioned if it is really related to the Bathsheba incident (2 Samuel 11 – 12), as the heading claims. There is, however, no need to question the accuracy and authenticity of the heading. The opening meditation on the wonder of repentance (Psalm 51:1–3) could so easily have arisen out of 2 Samuel 12:13. The agony of remorse reflected in Psalm 51:7–11 takes us into David's mind during his week of fasting and desperate anxiety (2 Samuel 12:15–17). The unexpected return to the theme of deliverance from sin in Psalm 51:14 finds its explanation in the fact that adultery and murder merited the death penalty under the law. The reference to the unavailability of a sacrifice acceptable to the Lord (Psalm 51:16) arises from the same source: no sacrifice was specified to cover adultery and murder. But David knew deep down that somewhere in the heart and plan of God, even these sins could find sprinkled blood sufficient to cleanse them – hence the plea for a 'purging with hyssop' (Psalm 51:7), referring back to Exodus 12:22. Finally, the perceived danger to Jerusalem (Psalm 51:18) required the involvement of a king. No ordinary citizen could be a public menace on this scale! Of course, Bathsheba and her sorely wronged husband Uriah are not named in the psalm, nor indeed are there any specific details of how the adultery came about or how the murder was committed. It would be against the genius of Hebrew poetry to do this. Psalm 51 brings us inside the story, and meditates not on its narrative development but on its spiritual significance.

Psalm 57

Psalm 57 (cf. Psalm 142) is a beautifully moving example of David's autobiographical meditation. He had two 'cave' experiences: 1 Samuel 22:1a and 1 Samuel 24. Only the former fits the details of these psalms. The first time he sought safety in a cave must have been a low ebb indeed in David's fortunes and feelings. After his secret anointing as king in 1 Samuel 16, events must surely have seemed to him a logical outworking of the Lord's plan: his welcome to Saul's court, his success against Goliath, and his national popularity. Surely kingship was within sight! But no, it was not the life of the court but the life of a fugitive that awaited him (1 Samuel 19:11). Even his home offered no security (1 Samuel 19:12ff.; Psalm 59). Not the palace, then, but the cave! And in the darkness, the growling and prowling of lions (Psalm 57:4). But then came one of David's 'epiphany moments'. He was in 'the cave', says the heading, but when he looked up into the darkness of its rocky roof he saw instead that he was actually 'in the shadow of your wings' (Psalm 57:1). The cave was all too real, at one level of experience, but the 'real reality', the story within the story, was the overshadowing wings which would remain 'until the disaster has passed' – and beyond!

Reading a psalm

Looking, as we have done, at a few of David's autobiographical psalms has taught us that biblical psalms set out to penetrate through to underlying spiritual realities, and to teach us how to live with those realities in the forefront of our thoughts, plans and enjoyments. The way the cave became the wings is a particularly good example of what the whole collection is about.

We can never read a psalm without profit, for there is always some verse or thought that is helpful, but to get the real benefit of a psalm, a little more work is usually needed. Like all true poetry, a psalm is not a haphazard jumble of thoughts, but a coherent expression of a truth or theme. We harvest the real fruit of a psalm when we discover what that central truth is, and then go on to discover the way it is presented, developed and applied.

Psalm 23
Psalm 23, for example, focuses our minds on three 'I will' truths:

▶ Verse 1, 'I will lack nothing.'

▶ Verse 4, 'I will fear no evil.'

▶ Verse 6, 'I will dwell in the house of the Lord for ever.'

It starts with the ongoing present: I am provided for. It moves to the unknown future: I am guarded. And it ends with the ultimate outcome: I will dwell in the house of the Lord. The Shepherd provides, guards and brings safely home. Many psalms have this 'shape', moving progressively forward, step by step, from beginning to end.

Psalm 78

The central thought of this psalm is the importance of remembering who the Lord is and what he has done, while forgetfulness brings failure. Following the introduction (Psalm 78:1–8), this is the leading thought in each of the two main sections of the psalm (verses 9–11, 'forgot'; 40–42, 'did not remember'), and it is developed in four parallels: the redeeming (12–14, 43–53), providing (15–16, 54–55), judging (17–33, 56–64) and loving (34–39, 65–72) Lord.

Psalm 67

A remarkable number of psalms have a 'circular' or chiastic pattern, moving by stages to a central thought, and then developing that central thought in matching stages. For example, Psalm 67 begins with a wish (a^1, verses 1–2), may 'God bless us', and ends (a^2, verses 6–7) with the confident 'God will bless us'. Verses 3 (b^1) and 6 (b^2) call for universal praise. The central thought (c, verse 4) is the affirmation that some glad day the Lord will 'judge' (NIV, inexplicably, 'rule') – that is, make those authoritative decisions which will 'set everything to rights' (cf. Psalms 96:11–13; 98:7–9).

The central truth of the whole book

All of life is in the Psalms. Life's troubles are candidly faced: depression (Psalms 42 – 43), inequalities and unfairnesses (72), pain without cure or hope (88). The writers wrestle with history and its meaning (78; 105 – 106), they probe present living (1) and coming death (49). In everything their eyes are on the Lord, bringing him their sins (51), their adoration (18:1–3), their unqualified praise (145; 150) and worship (100). They are keenly aware of his glory and greatness in creation (29; 104). Nothing is dodged: malicious tongues (59; 120), false friends (41), darkness in all its forms (120; 134), unexpected and undeserved trial (44), deadly dangers (124). The list is endless; everything is in the Psalms. The old hymn encouraged us to 'take it to the Lord in prayer'. The Psalms would say, more simply, 'take it to the Lord' – that is, 'angle' your life like a reflecting mirror so that whatever comes to you is at once reflected and deflected up into his presence, whether as prayer or praise, confession or adoration, bewilderment or delight, anger or laughter, the weeping that endures for a night or the joy that comes in the morning. Just 'take it to the Lord'.

Patterns, shapes and meaning: spend a week with the psalm of your choice

Give yourself a treat by probing deeply into the meaning of a psalm through working out its structure or shape. The following pointers are just to get you started, in the hope that the bug of Bible analysis will bite you deeply and permanently! Don't try to tackle all seven – unless you are on holiday, or retired! A whole week spent with any one of these would be a feast.

Day 1
Psalm 1 can be seen as circular, with the enduring fruit (verse 3) contrasted with the impermanent chaff (4) at its centre. Work out how verses 1 and 6, and verses 2 and 5 contrast with each other.

Day 2
Psalm 16 opens and closes (verses 1, 9–11) with the theme of security in God. Verses 2–8 list some evidence pointing to security in God. How can we be sure of our eternal security?

Day 3
Psalm 46: faith faces facts. Look at it as three moves: God in the storm (verses 1–3) ... in the city (4–7) ... in the whole earth (8–11).

Day 4
Psalm 59 is one of David's bits of autobiography. Read it along with 1 Samuel 19:10–18. Its theme is our total security in the Lord. 'Protect' (Psalm 59:1), and 'fortress' (verses 9, 16–17) share the idea of being lifted high above the threat. Learn how to deal with a time of stress, extreme pressure and threat.

Day 5
Psalm 100: a beautiful meditation on a caring Lord and his cherished people. Note three imperatives in verses 1–2 and 4, followed each time by three truths about the Lord (and his people).

Day 6
Psalm 124: the Lord is on our side. How many pictures of different threats – and divine rescue – can you find?

Day 7
Psalm 150: what a suitable (and marvellous) conclusion to the whole collection! Just a sustained shout of praise. So what is praise? Pretty well every verse gives part of the answer.

A skeleton in the cupboard

Surely not in the Psalms! Please! No!

Don't get too starry-eyed about the Psalms. Certainly it is a book to delight in, and to thank God for. But – be honest – do you feel like praying, 'Break the arm of the wicked' (Psalm 10:15)? And what about wishing for someone's sudden death (55:15), or that their children would become beggars (109:10)? Not to mention pronouncing 'happy' the person who dashes infants against rocks (137:8–9)!

Throughout the Old Testament

This is a real problem. There are about twenty-five places in the Psalms where our moral hackles are raised, and the bony fingers of this skeleton in the cupboard reach out into other parts of the Old Testament as well. The whole human race, except for one family, perished in the flood (Genesis 6:7, 17; 7:21–23); Jacob's matrimonial arrangements seem decidedly questionable (Genesis 29 – 30); Judah consorted with a prostitute – or thought he was doing so (Genesis 38); and Joshua obeyed the Lord by 'exterminating' the Canaanites 'without mercy' (Joshua 11:16–20).

And the New: a Bible problem

Before we review these 'moral problems' in the Psalms and the Old Testament, we must notice similar features in the New Testament. Jesus was pretty unsparing in his 'woe'-pronouncements (Matthew 23), and saw – and apparently accepted – that his second coming would involve consequences comparable to the flood (Matthew 24:37–39). The divine judgment on Ananias and Sapphira (Acts 5:1–11) seems as callous, in kind, as anything the Old Testament records; no 'curse' in the Psalms comes anywhere near Paul's anathema (Galatians 1:8–9), spoken as it is in the full knowledge of its eternal dimensions; under the heavenly altar martyred souls call out for vengeance, and are promised it (Revelation 6:9–11); and what about the 'lake of fire' in Revelation (Revelation 20:11–15)?

Back to the Old Testament

As we turn, then, to what are called the 'moral problems in the Old Testament', it is well to keep in mind that in the whole Bible, not to mention also on the lips of Jesus, we find material that is at first sight unacceptable, even offensive. If it seems more abundant in the Old Testament, remember that the Old is so much larger than the New! It is also the case that the Old Testament records more of the history of men and nations, and, if it did not accurately reflect the sort of things that happen in this sorry world, the same people who now accuse it of being bloodthirsty would accuse it of being unrealistic!

The following classification of 'moral problems in the Old Testament' is offered, not as all-inclusive, but to sketch out a method of approach, or at the very least to show that there are two sides to this, as to every question.

Problems to be met in a spirit of faith

Events involving colossal loss of life are presented in the Bible as well-merited judgments visited by a holy God after careful inquiry:

▶ The flood (Genesis 6:5–7).

117

▶ The destruction of Sodom (Genesis 18:20–21).

▶ The fall of the northern (2 Kings 17:7–23) and southern (2 Kings 24:3–4) kingdoms.

To be sure, we cannot be insensitive to such loss of life, with its attendant sufferings and sadnesses, but the Bible has not kept it as a dark secret that such things are the inevitable outcome of sin. The real question is whether we believe that 'the Judge of all the earth' does 'right' (Genesis 18:24). This is the Bible's 'world-view', what life is like in a world of sinners under the rule of a sovereign and holy God. Do we believe it?

Think, for example, of the plague that followed David's census (2 Samuel 24). We do not know why 'numbering the people' was counted such a menacing thing, but even a hard-headed customer like Joab knew it was wrong (verse 3), and tried in vain to restrain the king. In the outcome, David spoke for all of us: 'I am the one who has sinned … These are but sheep. What have they done?' But, according to verse 1, they had done plenty! What aroused the Lord's anger we are not told, but, whatever it was, this was his chosen way of dealing with the offence given. Do we believe that the Judge of all the earth does right?

But what about Joshua, slaughtering the Canaanites, right, left and centre, at the Lord's command (e.g. Joshua 11:16–20)? Again, we are called to adopt a position of faith. Genesis 15:6, 15–16 is a case history of the way God rules the world with moral integrity. Abram has been brought out of Ur specifically to possess Canaan (Genesis 15:7), but he cannot have it until four generations have passed, because 'the sin of the Amorites has not yet reached its full measure' (verse 16). In other words, 'Yes, you are going to possess this land, but I could only give it to you now if I took it, without cause, from its rightful owners. This would be an injustice, and I cannot do it. I am therefore putting the Amalekite population on 400 years' moral probation. When they fail their probation, and are ripe for judgment, your descendants can justly dispossess them.'

To say that this is precisely what happened is in no way to gloss over the grimness of the task of social surgery given to Joshua, but it does teach us that there is no reaping without sowing and ripening (cf. Galatians 6:7; Revelation 14:17–20). The Judge of all the earth does right.

Problems to be met in a spirit of sorrow

There are cases in the Old Testament where people's mistakes besmirch the good name of the Lord. Such a case is 2 Samuel 21:1–14. Three years of famine prompted inquiry as to whether some specific sin lay behind this calamity (2 Samuel 21:1), and it transpired that Saul had broken faith with the Gibeonites (cf. Joshua 9). Saul's act is not recorded, but obviously it was known to David, and rankling with the Gibeonites. David made serious mistakes in his response. First, he asked, not the Lord (cf. Joshua 9:14) but the Gibeonites what should be done, and they demanded human sacrifice. Secondly, beyond belief, David granted their request (2 Samuel 21:6)! This, of course, was not God's way of dealing with sin. David did not go the way of repentance. He did not seek out some atoning sacrifice. He did not make a direct appeal for forgiveness. Rather, he violated the mind of God, who, in Genesis 22, ruled out human sacrifice, and provided a substitutionary alternative (2 Samuel 21:13; cf. Exodus 13:13). He disobeyed the explicit command of God (Deuteronomy 24:16) that fathers shall not be put to death for their children or vice versa, and he broke his own promise to Saul (1 Samuel 24:21–22) not to put his family to death. What a catalogue of misjudgment! In 2 Samuel 21:14, 'after that' must not for a moment be taken to mean that the Lord turned to favour his people as a result of such an appalling catalogue of mistakes. 'After that' (*'aḥărê-kēn*) means 'afterwards' or 'subsequently'. It is a preposition of sequence, not of causation. As the NIV says, 'God answered prayer', just as he would have done at the start, without David's gruesome, cruel and sinful decisions.

A similar case of human sacrifice is recorded in 2 Kings 3. A coalition of Israel, Judah and Edom attacked Moab, and the Moabite forces made a last stand in Kir Hareseth. When a desperate situation demanded desperate measures, the king of Moab 'took his firstborn son ... and offered him as a sacrifice on the city wall' (2 Kings 3:27). This resulted in 'fury against Israel' and the coalition broke up in disarray. A usual interpretation of this is that the king of Moab offered his own son, and by this costly sacrifice secured God's favour. The sheer monstrousness of the suggestion that the Lord would be won over by such a deed should make commentators re-examine the passage in question. When verse 27 says 'his firstborn son', in the context 'his' must refer to the king of Edom mentioned at the end of verse 26. A different picture now emerges. During the course of the war, as we may presume, Edom's son and heir was taken prisoner. At the height of the crisis, the lad was killed publicly on the city wall. In consequence, Moab turned in fury on the king of Israel (the prime mover in the war, verse 6), and the coalition (an unlikely alliance at the best of times) dissolved under the strain.

Problems to be met in a spirit of fear

There are incidents in the Old Testament, often classed as problematical, where a thoughtful reaction would be to show reverential fear rather than find cause for complaint. In 1 Samuel 4, the ark of the covenant, accompanying the army of Israel, was captured by the Philistines. But if Israel erred in thinking of the ark as a 'lucky mascot' (4:3) which they could manipulate to their advantage, the Philistines erred by thinking of it as a mere religious ornament (5:1–2) which could as well decorate Dagon's shrine as the Lord's. The Lord vented his anger on the Philistines (5:1–12) and rescued the ark. In this way, it arrived at Beth Shemish (6:10–12). The resulting joy and sacrifice were understandable and proper (6:13–15), but the Beth Shemites sinned by (literally) 'looking at' the ark (cf. Numbers 4:15, 20), and they were struck down (there is some uncertainty in the text as to the number) by divine judgment (1 Samuel 6:19).

If there are those today who find such divine action repugnant, it is important to note that this was not the reaction at Beth Shemish. There 'the people mourned because of the heavy blow the Lord had dealt them, and ... asked, "Who can stand in the presence of the LORD, this holy God?"' (1 Samuel 6:20).

But there's more. David wanted to bring up the ark from obscurity at Kiriath Jearim (1 Samuel 7:1; 2 Samuel 6:2–3; Psalm 132:3–6) to his newly established capital city. En route to Jerusalem, Uzzah touched the ark (2 Samuel 6:6) and was struck down on the spot. David was outraged, as well he might have been (verse 8). For that is the natural reaction of human logic. What, after all, does it matter if some pettifogging regulation is transgressed? This is not, however, a biblically instructed reaction. The ark is one of the covenant sacraments of the Old Testament, an effective sign of the Lord's presence, and, indeed, of his saving mercies, and he will not allow his covenant signs to be tampered with: they are holy, as he is.

How easily today we overlook Paul's assertion that misuse of the Lord's Supper is deadly (1 Corinthians 11:2–30). How casually we fail adequately to 'fence' the Lord's Table. How unthinkingly we allow baptism to become a social convention. Sometimes, as with Uzzah, or with Ananias and Sapphira (Acts 5), the Lord lets us see how seriously he views an offence, so that we may adjust our thinking and conduct accordingly.

It is the Philistines, who know no better, who put the ark on a cart (1 Samuel 6:7ff.). David, under the Word of God (Numbers 4:5–6, 15; Joshua 3:6, 13), should know better. Philistines can look at the ark, even handle it, but the men of Beth Shemish, David and Uzzah, have been instructed differently by the Word of God. And, instead of criticizing what the Old Testament records, we should learn with them to stand in awe, and to revere the holy God (1 Samuel 6:20; 2 Samuel 6:9), respect his ordinances and keep his commandments.

We must glance at one other example of 'problems to be met in a spirit of fear': Elisha and the bears in 2 Kings 2:23–25. The story seems one of gross over-reaction. An elderly, bald-headed prophet is faced by some unthinking youngsters who mock his shining pate. But he happens to have a short fuse – and his God has an even shorter one! We are not helped, either, by the Authorized Version which says that the mockers were 'little children', creating the impression that, as ill luck would have it, Elisha arrived at Bethel just as the local playgroup was out in the garden having its mid-morning milk!

What, however, are the facts of the story if we consider them more thoughtfully? First, Elisha was not elderly, but a young man who had recently taken on the mantle of Elijah and become senior prophet in Israel. Secondly, the AV's phrase 'little children' (NIV 'youths'; Hebrew *nĕ'ārîm qĕṭannîm*) has a wide spread of use: it can mean 'children', maybe even 'a baby' (2 Kings 5:14), but we find it used of any age under responsible adulthood (1 Kings 3:7), of a 'teenager' acting as an attendant (1 Samuel 20:35), and of a resolute leader well in charge of things (1 Kings 11:17). In other words, it means those who are 'on the young side', but their actual age and description must suit the context. The noun *na'ar* by itself is used of the men of Abram's private army in Genesis 14:24, and of the seventeen years of Joseph in Genesis 37:2. The different word *yĕlādîm*, translated 'children' (AV) or 'youths' (NIV) in 2 Kings 2:24, is used of Rehoboam and his contemporaries in 1 Kings 12:8, 10, 14 at a time when Rehoboam was forty-one (1 Kings 14:21). Here again, in 2 Kings 2, the word must reflect the age range suited to the context.

With some gentle reading between the lines, then, and a little bit of imagination, a more persuasive story emerges. It is understandable that Bethel would arrange a hostile reception committee for Elisha. He was the brand new prophet in Israel, no longer Elijah's assistant but his successor – the leader, as we might say, of 'the Lord's work' – the one on whom the continuing prophetic voice of the

Lord depended. Bethel, however, was the headquarters of an ancient heresy (1 Kings 12:22–29). Sound policy dictated landing the first blow. So the priests of Bethel 'rented a mob' of what the NIV politely calls 'youths', but who might more accurately be called 'louts' or 'young thugs', to taunt the prophet and see him off. There is no explanation as to why the chant of 'baldhead' was insulting. Indeed, it is unlikely that, even if Elisha were bald, he would be out and about with his head uncovered. Could it rather be that this is a case, still common enough, of mockery by contrast? Children still call bald men 'hairy' or 'curly'. Maybe, from under Elisha's head-covering, the flowing, uncut locks of Nazarene consecration to God were evident (Numbers 6:5), and the devotees of Jeroboam's bulls were mocking his devotion to the Lord. In any case, what is Elisha to do, faced by a hostile mob? Either to run or to stand and fight would equally spell the end of his ministry. Error would have challenged him and won. There is, however, a third way: to call on his God, which he did, with dramatic results.

We may well ask: if the bears 'mauled forty-two' louts, how many were there in the mob to begin with, and how many escaped unscathed? For certain, two or three times that number. But be that as it may, the central question prompted by the incident is this: What sort of God do we want and need? A God who is not there when we pray (cf. 1 Kings 18:26–28), or a God who is ready, willing and mighty to save, possessing every resource to do so, and acting with an exactness of justice that befits the Judge of all the earth?

Problems to be met in a spirit of humility

We come now to the point where we started: the 'imprecatory psalms', and how we are to understand them. Many commentators say that verses like Psalm 10:15 and the rest are just evidence of 'Old Testament morality', which we have left behind under the influence of Jesus and the New Testament. This simply will not do.

▶ First, it overlooks the presence (as we saw) of similar material in the New Testament, and on the lips of Jesus.

▶ Secondly, Old Testament morality is not like that. It forbids taking vengeance, bearing grudges, and cherishing enmity in the heart (Leviticus 19:17–18). Contrast, for example, David's behaviour to the sick slave and that of his Amalekite master who left him to die (1 Samuel 30:11–14), or note the enviable reputation that Israelite kings enjoyed (1 Kings 20:31), or the Old Testament's teaching on accepting hurt and refusing to get one's own back (Psalm 35:12–14; Proverbs 20:22; 24:29; 25:21–22).

▶ But, thirdly, to set these verses aside as 'Old Testament morality' would be untrue to the very psalms in which they are found, for, in almost every case, alongside the imprecations lie verses proving that we are dealing with a writer of the deepest spirituality and devotion to the Lord. Psalm 139 is a case in point, where following the most exalted theology, and a spirit delighting in the fact that there is no escaping from this great God (verses 1–18), there is a dire prayer for the destruction of the wicked (19–22). Do we dismiss David as a hypocrite, pretending to the spirituality of the opening verses? Or was he a schizoid personality whose thoughts Godward and manward were at war with each other? Or do we just smile indulgently over the fact that even the best are still sinners? Or is it possible that David's morality had a wholeness we have lost and should seek to recover? Should we summon ourselves to humility rather than superiority?

A more positive understanding of the imprecations must start by noting that (apart from Psalm 137:8–9, see below) *all the imprecations are prayers*. They are in fact a particular example of what the Psalms as a whole are all about: take it to the Lord. There is no indication that the psalmists contemplated personal vengeance, and we have no right even to assume a malignant spirit animating their prayers. Indeed, the serene spirituality of their psalms forbids us to think such a thing. They were in dire difficulty, and they took it to the Lord in prayer. This is a mark of true, consistent godliness. How often it is the case with us that once we prayed, formerly attended church, used to believe – until trouble struck! But here are people in severe, sometimes savage, trial, and *all they did was bring their problem vigorously into the presence of the Lord – and leave it there!*

But such prayers! Surely they cannot be right. Break their arms (Psalm 10:15), their teeth (58:6), make their food a snare and their homes empty (69:22, 25), blot them out of the book of life (69:28), make their days few and their children orphans (109:8–9)? Surely it's all much more than a bit over the top. This is a serious charge and merits a serious answer.

First, even if it should be the case that such prayers are in themselves wrong, surely better a wrong prayer than a stab in the back, better a private imprecation than a terrorist's explosive. In any troubled spot in the world, wouldn't a sinful prayer be an improvement on guns and maiming? In every private hostility, would not a mistaken prayer which left the matter at that be better than vendettas, animosity and inflicted hurtfulness?

But, secondly, and more importantly, rather than calling these prayers 'wrong' we should call them 'realistic'. For example, we find no difficulty in Psalm 143:11, 'Bring me out of trouble', but we criticize verse 12, 'Destroy all my foes'. But surely, rather, we should extend to David the courtesy of assuming that in the circumstances then prevailing, there was no other way out of his trouble except the downfall of his enemies? And is it not equally the case today that when we pray blandly for the deliverance of Christians wrongly maltreated by oppressive governments, we are asking for the overthrow of those regimes (but backing away from saying so). Today coolness is in, moral rigour and outrage are out. The psalmists were more finely tuned to the holiness and wrath of a sin-hating God.

This brings us to a third fact relating to the imprecations. Even in human courts, the Lord decreed that an unjust accuser should be sentenced to whatever he had wished to visit on the other party (Deuteronomy 19:16–19). This accounts for much of the realism of the imprecations. If the psalmists prayed broadly for vindication, they knew that in fact they were asking God to visit on their accusers the penalty of their unjust accusations. And in every situation, the God who forbids us to take vengeance promises vengeance. This is the way things work in his world: no good ever goes unrewarded, no fault unpunished. It may not look like that, but that's the way it is. God rules in holiness and justice, and vengeance 'belongs' to him (Deuteronomy 32:35; Psalm 94:1; Romans 12:19).

This moral view of the world lies behind Psalm 137:8–9 where translators, sadly, have not been our best friends. The word which the NIV translates 'happy' (cf. ESV 'blessed') is the Hebrew *'ašrê*. A concordance shows that it is capable of three shades of meaning: under God's blessing (e.g. Psalm 32:1), personally fulfilled (e.g. 1:1), and 'right', doing the right thing in a given situation (e.g. 106:3). This third meaning is, in fact, the one most in accord with the basic sense of the word, for it comes from the verb *'āšar*, 'to go straight', and it is the only meaning that suits Psalm 137. We may put it this way: in God's world, this is what Babylon gave, therefore this is what Babylon will *rightly* get. The verses (please note) are a statement of fact, not of wish, preference or request. They express the quid pro quo which is the basic principle of God's absolute justice.

'In your anger, do not sin,' says Paul (Ephesians 4:26). Realism bids us respond, 'Easier said than done!' At least part of our problem with the imprecations is that we know that if we were to pray like that, our hearts would be infected with feelings of vengeful animosity and maybe real hatred of our foes. There is nothing in the Psalms in question which allows us to impute such feelings to their writers; rather, everything leads us to the opposite conclusion. They express on these occasions a pure anger in which there was no sin, an anger reflecting what Revelation calls 'the wrath of the Lamb' (6:16), and of which there was an instance in Matthew 23.

Prayer in the Psalms: A thought a day for seven days

Day 1
Psalm 4:1: The verse begins and ends by asking God to hear our prayer. He is a God who does what is right, sends relief and acts in mercy.

Day 2
Psalm 25:4–7: Faced with triumphalist enemies (verse 2), David's prayer is for guidance and instruction. Note the contrast: 'remember ... remember not ...'

Day 3
Psalm 38: Does this psalm belong to the same time as Psalm 51? Meditate on David's remorse, ill repute, suffering and loss, consequent on his sin with Bathsheba. When the Lord is justly angry with us, we can pray against his anger (38:1). When our basic problem is that we have alienated him, we can pray for his quick return to us (38:21–22).

Day 4
Psalm 86:1–7: Grounds on which prayer can be made: personal need (verse 1), personal faith (2), persistent prayer (3), appeal to the Lord alone (4), his forgiveness and love (5), his mercy (6), the trouble we are in (7).

Day 5
Psalm 116:1–7: The benefits that answered prayer brings.

Day 6
Psalm 123: Verse 1, my eyes, his throne; verse 2, my eyes,

his hand. Prayer is submitting to his kingliness (verse 1), his absolute ownership of us (2a), his timetable ('till', 2), his assessment of how much we are able to endure (3). The world may scorn, but it is our resource to pray (4).

Day 7
Psalm 143:7–10: There are seven separate prayers here, and six reasons for praying. Over to you!

Question

Is there a 'moral problem' in the Old Testament that you still wrestle with? How would you explain its presence in the Bible to someone who is worried about it? How would you explain it to a non-Christian who is just exploring the Bible for the first time?

Five self-portraits

About a fifth of the Bible is taken up by the books of the prophets. It's very likely that if we were to close our eyes and visualize the Old Testament, it would be all those acres of print that would spring to mind. Not only this, but, if we turn from visualizing to listening, maybe we would think we overheard, in the distance, rather demagogic voices shouting denunciations!

In the news

We need to beware of living with such cartoon-like impressions and popular misconceptions. Far from being just acres of print, the prophets were the headline-makers of their day. Amos had a deportation order served on him because his preaching was thought likely to disrupt a whole kingdom, and in any case unsuitable for the Chapel Royal (Amos 7:10–13)! Elijah had the police out hunting him (1 Kings 18:10). Haggai changed the course of government (Haggai 1:1–2, 12). Ezekiel was more than a bit eccentric (Ezekiel 4:4–6; 12:3–6), and Isaiah had his moments too (Isaiah 20:2–3). Jeremiah became a sort of Public Enemy No. 1 (Jeremiah 15:10). They were far from being the dull, incomprehensible, negative sober-sides we imagine, and if we find them so the fault must be ours, not theirs.

Amos and the call of God (Amos 7:10–17)

Five of the prophets leave us personal testimonies of their call. Taking them in date order, we start with Amos. Politically speaking, Jeroboam (Amos 7:10; 2 Kings 14:23–29; 786–746 BC) was one of the great kings of Israel. Under him, the kingdom once more reached the territorial dimensions it had enjoyed under Solomon, and society was exceedingly prosperous, although with wealth unequally shared out (Amos 2:6; 4:1–3). Jonah had predicted a restored kingdom (2 Kings 14:25); Amos predicted its demise (Amos 2:6–16; 3:11; 7:10–11). No wonder, then, that he was opposed by the establishment who would gladly have seen the back of him (7:12–13). Amos' reply, while in no way mealy-mouthed or apologetic, was quiet and reasoned – indeed we will never fully enter into the book of Amos until we learn to read it as a reasoned argument, spoken with quiet and even tearful persuasiveness.

He was not a prophet by personal choice (Amos 7:14, literally, 'I was not a prophet'), nor by training in the prophetic schools ('nor a prophet's son', cf. 2 Kings 6:1, where NIV 'company' is literally 'sons'). Professionally, he was a stockman (NIV 'shepherd') and cultivated low-grade sycamore-figs used as cattle feed (Amos 7:14). But into this very ordinary life there intruded, seemingly abruptly, the call of God (verse 15).

Amos could hardly have expressed his sense of divine compulsion more strongly: 'The Lord took me', he says (Amos 7:15), using the verb (*lāqaḥ*) which describes Elijah being snatched from earth to heaven (2 Kings 2:2, 5, 9–10; cf. Psalm 49:15). Very likely the word 'prophet' itself (*nābî'*) means 'someone sent', and Amos' new calling involved 'going' and 'saying'. It may be that he already knew some of the towns of northern Israel, even Samaria itself (1 Kings 16:24, 29), as markets for his wool and figs, but in any case he must now leave Tekoa and become a prophet to Israel, the northern kingdom.

Prophecy was basically the marvel of being able to say,

'This is what the Lord has said' (Amos 7:17, literally), or, as Amos 1:1, 3 spells it out: 'The words of Amos ... This is what the Lord has said.' Fuller discussion of this must wait till we come to Ezekiel's self-portrait, but Amos claims what all the prophets would claim: that the words were his own, each prophet speaking in his own distinctive style, using the words that came naturally to him. But each prophet actually said what the Lord himself would have said had he chosen to be there in his own person. Amos' words were the Lord's words; the Lord said what Amos said. This is the miracle of prophecy.

Hosea and the broken heart of God (Hosea 1 – 3)

Amos became a prophet there and then, on that day when the Lord 'took' him. Meditating on seven or so turbulent and ultimately heartbreaking years within his own home and family, Hosea might have said, 'I have become a prophet.' At any rate, this is one way of interpreting how Hosea portrays himself, how he discovered by hindsight that all the twists and turns of his experience were in fact what the Lord was saying to Israel.

Commentators dispute how we are to understand Hosea's autobiography (Hosea 1:2–9; 3:1–5). Some even deny any connection between the chapters, holding them to be two distinct stories of two distinct relationships. This, however, would contradict what the Hebrew of 3:1 actually says. We should translate it not as 'Go yet love', as in KJV (cf. NKJV, ESV), but 'Go ... love ... again' as in NIV. The adverb, 'again', belongs with the main verb 'love', not with the auxiliary verb 'go' It is a command to renew an existing love, not to form a new alliance. Behind this command lies his broken heart; out of this command arises his message of undying love and hope.

It is not possible to be certain what sort of girl Hosea married. She is called (1:2, literally) 'a wife of harlotry/ prostitution', and at first sight that seems to put the matter beyond doubt, but the parallel expression, 'children of harlotry/prostitution' opens the question again. Hosea could not guarantee ahead of time that children would be born in his house of whom he was not the father (though, in the event, his paternity is only actually asserted of his firstborn, 1:3; contrast 1:6, 8). Maybe the way Gomer is described means nothing more than 'a typical Israelite girl, of the time', for the worship of Baal, or worshipping the Lord as if he were Baal, was rife in Israel.

Baal-worship depended on 'sympathetic' or 'imitative' magic, and the easiest way to understand this is to think how a parent tries to teach a toddler to blow its nose! It is too early for verbal instruction or appeal, so what we do is hold a handkerchief to the needy organ and make nose-blowing noises, hoping (often successfully) that the infant will imitate us. Bingo!

Since Baal was not a person but an impersonal power of fertilization, he could not be reasoned with, and the only recourse was to do on earth whatever you wanted Baal to imitate in heaven, hoping that he would see and 'get the idea' (see pp. 145–146 below). For this reason, Baal-worship was noisy (to catch his attention) and performed on high places (so that he could see what was going on). 'Baal' was in fact a sort of shorthand for what we would call 'market forces', which in an agricultural economy meant plenty of sons (to run the farm) and daughters (to marry off to other farmers' sons and thus increase the acreage) and a good annual return on crops and animals. This understandable emphasis on fertility meant that 'worship' involved the public performance of human fertilizing acts, hoping to stimulate Baal to do the same, and every Baal-shrine had to guarantee a supply of men and women for sexual purposes. Within a Baalized society this would be taken for granted. Such sexual activity was an expression of devotion to this god. Indeed, in Genesis 38:21, such a girl is called (literally) a 'holy woman' (*qĕdēšâ*), that is, one separated off to the service of the god who demanded such conduct. Socially this 'Baalized sex' was part (so to speak) of 'going to church on Sunday'. It was the way things were. The Bible, of course, bluntly calls it harlotry, departing from the Lord to become a prostitute.

Reading between the lines, Hosea's 'story' comes out like this. He married Gomer (Hosea 1:3), a typical girl of the time, and three children (verses 3–8) were born within the marriage. But at some point Hosea became aware of her ongoing infidelity, and at some point Gomer left the marital home. This scenario suits the way Hosea applies his situation to Israel in the name of the Lord (e.g. 2:2, 4–5).

It would be strange if in these circumstances Hosea did not begin to question whether he had been right to marry her in the first place. But the answer he got was unequivocal. He was not only right, but had been divinely directed into this sad marriage. Why, that was actually the beginning of the Lord's word to him (Hosea 1:2). The Lord had led him into all this personal grief and domestic turmoil. It was all part of a plan.

So what next? Does 2:5–6 suggest the possibility that Gomer was wearying of her footloose life and considering coming home? And if so, what was Hosea to do now? Once more the answer is unequivocal: Hosea must do what the Lord does. He must love Gomer the way the Lord loves Israel (3:1). Within his own heartbreaking home circumstances, Hosea learns of the broken heart of the Lord, and is called to live according to the same broken-heart pattern, and to go on loving his unfaithful wife with an undying love.

Mystery and miracle

How very differently, then, the word of the Lord 'came' to his chosen mouthpieces. In the case of Amos, 'the Lord said' (Amos 7:15), but Hosea himself 'became' the word. It was 'made flesh' in him, his home and family. Even his children were given names expressing God's word (Hosea 1:4–5, 6–7, 8–9). In their own persons they were what God was saying, and when Gomer was accepted back, it was an expression of the Lord's patient, unceasing, ever-renewed love for his harlot people.

But how the Lord 'spoke' his revealed word, and

inspired his chosen servants, the prophets, to communicate it, is never told. Mostly the Hebrew Bible simply says 'the word of the LORD came' (e.g. Jeremiah 1:4). 'Came' here represents the verb 'to be' – 'the word ... was to ...' or, expressing more exactly what the verb 'to be' means in Hebrew, 'the word of the Lord became a living/present reality to ...' We learn of an amazing fact, but not of how it happened. For the most part the prophets do not go beyond 'the Lord said' or 'the word of the Lord came'. Sometimes the Lord 'spoke' through experiences, as with Hosea (e.g. Jeremiah 18:1–5), sometimes through dreams (e.g. Jeremiah 31:26; Daniel 7:1), sometimes through 'visions' (e.g. Isaiah 6:1; Zechariah 1:8), but always the mystery and the miracle remain.

So, how does God speak?

▶ *Revelation:* God making his word known to his chosen agents.

▶ *Inspiration:* God making it possible for them to express his word in their own words, while at the same time remaining true to themselves and using their own characteristic forms of speech, the product of their own thought-processes.

Isaiah and the holiness of God

From one point of view, then, Amos and Hosea were unique, in the way they received and spoke the word of God. From another point of view, they were very ordinary: Amos with his farm, Hosea with his marriage breakdown. This helps us to see that what James (5:17) says about Elijah is true of all the prophets: they were 'just like us'. The same is true of Isaiah, Jeremiah and Ezekiel, though it is rather their spiritual affinity with us that comes to the fore.

> O how shall I, whose native sphere
> Is dark, whose mind is dim,

> Before the Ineffable appear,
> And on my naked spirit bear
> the uncreated beam?

The words are those of Thomas Binney (in his hymn 'Eternal Light'), but the experience was central to Isaiah's call to be a prophet (6:1–13), the day he found himself confronted by the highly exalted God and overheard the heavenly choir as it sang, 'Holy, Holy, Holy'.

We learn three things in turn about the Lord's holiness. First, that it is a unique holiness. Hebrew uses repetition to express what is superlative of its sort and the complete truth about something. In Genesis 14:10, 'full of … pits' is, literally, 'pits pits', the truth about the Valley of Siddim; in Deuteronomy 16:20, 'justice and justice alone' is, literally, 'righteousness righteousness', that is, 'true righteousness', 'the highest righteousness'. But in the whole of the Old Testament only one quality is 'raised to the power of three', the Lord's holiness. It is genuine holiness, it is the single all-embracing truth about God, and it is a super-superlative holiness.

Secondly, it is ethical holiness. In itself the word 'holy' probably means 'separate, different, other', but in the case of the God of Israel, what makes him 'separate, different and other' is his moral quality. In Isaiah 6 this is brought out by Isaiah's two simultaneous experiences. As soon as the Lord's holiness is proclaimed, the vision is withdrawn from Isaiah's gaze by clouds of smoke (verse 4), and he finds himself gripped by a conviction of sin and its ruinous penalty (5a). The Lord's holiness is more than a passive attribute, it is an active force, judging, expelling and destroying whatever offends it, even sins of speech (5b), something which we might consider petty, but which Isaiah knew to spell ruination.

How wonderful, therefore, that, thirdly, this is a saving holiness! In verses 6–7 the seraph comes to tell Isaiah about guilt taken away and sin atoned for, but 'seraph' means 'a burning one', and he came bearing a fiery ember. 'Fire' symbolizes the active, judging, death-dealing holiness of the Lord. In other words, when the Lord forgives sin, he does not cease to be himself in all his super-superlative, fiery holiness. But Isaiah makes a special point of noting that this particular burning ember came from the altar, the divinely appointed place where the fire of holiness burnt itself out and satisfied its demands on a substitutionary offering. This is not 'purification by fire' (hardly an Old Testament idea at all), but rather on the day he discovered freshly just how holy the Lord is, Isaiah also discovered how effective was the substitutionary sacrifice the Lord provided (Leviticus 17:11) to bring atonement and forgiveness, for through that forgiveness Isaiah is brought near enough (Isaiah 6:8) to the highly exalted God (verse 1) to overhear what he is saying, and he offers himself to be the Lord's prophet.

Jeremiah and the eternal plan of God

Jeremiah was quite different from Isaiah. Jeremiah never wanted to be a prophet (1:6), while Isaiah gives us the impression of never wanting to be anything else. The contrast extends to the way they were called to their work. Isaiah's call was full of drama, majesty, colour and movement, while Jeremiah's was low-key and private – the unexplained 'coming' of the word of God (1:4), the voice which revealed Jeremiah's pre-history (1:5), and which quietly over-ruled Jeremiah's reluctance (1:6–7). The hand gently 'touched' – the same verb as Isaiah's 'live coal' (Isaiah 6:7) – but how different, gentle and personal the touch! And with the touch came the promise that the very words of God were now in his mouth (Jeremiah 1:9).

It is clear from his book than none of this ever made Jeremiah *feel* any different. He still had to be cautioned against letting his fear master him (1:17); he still needed the comfort of God (8:18); he endured human enmity (11:19; 15:10); he still wearied of the demands of his work (12:5), and wrestled with the inscrutable ways of the Lord (20:7). In other words, his position was one of believing the promises God made to him, and acting in the obedience of faith.

In particular, the Lord let Jeremiah into the secret that he was God's man, long prepared, made ready for the times, already fitted and kitted for whatever he was now called to do. Even before conception (Jeremiah 1:5a) he was 'known' by the Lord (cf. Exodus 33:12–13, 17; Psalm 1:6); during the months of gestation (Jeremiah 1:5b) he was 'set apart' for God (literally, 'I sanctified you'); and, from the moment of birth, he was the Lord's prophet (verse 5b). This is primarily a wonderful statement of the far-seeing sovereignty of God in claiming us for himself (Ephesians 1:4; 1 Peter 1:1), but it also bears on the special function of the prophets to speak 'God's words' (Jeremiah 1:9). How can a person not just pass on the 'drift' of God's ideas but actually speak God's Word in God's words without becoming some sort of depersonalized tape-recorder or computer? The prophets (and the apostles after them, 1 Corinthians 2:12–13) were so prepared by divine predestination that what they said, naturally and in their individually characteristic fashion, was also what the Lord would have said if he had chosen to be there in his own person.

Maybe the illustration of a stained-glass window will help. Outside exists what we may call pure sunlight. Inside, that pure light is broken into the colours and patterns of the window. This, however, does not distort or spoil the light, or make it less pure than it was, for the colours and patterns of the window were designed by its creator to do just what they have done, filtering the sunlight to tell a story. So the prophets, God's long-prepared men, were filters of his truth, each imparting the intended colorations and emphases natural to his personality, and to his ways of thought and speech. In this way the pure Word of God, without loss of any of its purity, was spoken by his chosen agents as he himself would have spoken it (2 Timothy 3:14–16; 2 Peter 1:21).

But more of this when we consider Ezekiel. Isaiah was the man saved by the merits and efficacy of substitutionary sacrifice (cf. Romans 3:23–24; Ephesians 1:4, 7); Jeremiah exemplifies divine fore-planning, sovereign choice and individual preparation of those whom he has determined to make his own (Ephesians 1:4; 2:10). What he calls us to, he has long since prepared us for.

Ezekiel and the Word of God

The Lord's preparation of Jeremiah was age-long and secret. His preparation of Ezekiel, as it is recorded for us, was more like a tutorial course. Jeremiah's call is written in two or three verses while Ezekiel's covers at least chapters 1 – 3. Here is a running outline of the Lord's training course:

The Lord reveals himself, and speaks to Ezekiel (1:1 – 2:2).

⇩

Ezekiel is to speak God's Word to all (2:3–7).

⇩

Ezekiel is to hold God's Word in his heart and mouth (2:8 – 3:3).

⇩

The Word of God is Ezekiel's only and sufficient equipment (3:4–9).

⇩

Ezekiel is to hold God's Word in his heart and mouth (3:10–15).

⇩

Ezekiel is to speak God's Word to all (3:16–21).

⇩

The Lord reveals himself, and speaks to Ezekiel (3:22–27).

The whole sequence is held together by the recurring address to Ezekiel as 'son of man' (Ezekiel 2:3, 8; 3:4, 10, 17, 25), and by the constant emphasis on the Lord's Word (2:4, 7; 3:1, 4, 10–11, 17, 27). 'Son of man' underlines that Ezekiel is 'genuinely human', an 'ordinary' human being. The other emphasis, his responsibility to minister the Word of God, comes to a climax in 2:8 – 3:3.

Begin at Ezekiel 2:7 with its command to 'speak my words'. Note the plural: not just the general sense of what the Lord reveals, but the precise words the Lord would use. Now look at 3:4, the opening command of the next session in the Lord's training school, literally (cf. NKJV, ESV), 'speak with my words'. 'With' here is instrumental: literally, 'speak by (means of) my words'. These two commands bracket what happens in 2:6 – 3:3. Ezekiel has been given not just the Word of God but the words of God, and they are his sole and sufficient instrument of ministry. Objectively, the Word of God was:

▶ Given (2:9), a gift from God, handed over by God

▶ Complete (2:10a), a scroll written on both sides, leaving no room for any addition.

▶ Plain in its meaning (2:10b), grim though that meaning was in lament, mourning and woe.

▶ Brought home to the prophet by the act of God (3:2): literally, 'he caused me to eat'.

Subjectively,

▶ Ezekiel must be the first to obey the Word (2:8). He receives the Word, not as a tape-recorder would, but as a moral agent, responsible, commanded to be 'exhibit A' in obedience.

▶ Ezekiel must be the first to read and understand (2:10). The Lord made himself into a sort of lectern, holding the unrolled scroll until Ezekiel had read it from beginning to end and mastered its contents.

▶ Ezekiel must be to the first to accept the Word of God (3:2a) and enjoy its sweetness (3:3b).

There, in a nutshell, or rather, in an edible scroll, is all the Bible ever tells us about revelation (the gift of the Word of God) and inspiration (the enabling of this 'ordinary human being' to receive and understand it).

We can identify with so much of Ezekiel's experience:

the Word of God, the holy Scriptures, are God's gift to us, complete and entire, allowing neither addition nor subtraction, plain in meaning, to be read and understood, obeyed and loved. But Ezekiel, like all the prophets and apostles, was also unique, and in this we can rejoice but not identify with him. The Word of God was given to him in such a way that he was enabled to 'speak my words ... speak by means of my words'. This is the marvel and miracle of verbal inspiration, God's Word in God's words.

A thought a day for seven days on 'Man's mouth, God's Word'

Day 1
Exodus 4:12–15; 6:30 – 7:2. No explanation is ever given of how revelation (the gift of God's revealed Word) and inspiration (enabling people to receive and communicate it) work. But this is what God promised to Moses and Aaron, and what he did for his prophets.

Day 2
Deuteronomy 18:9–18. The Lord's people are to keep clear of all occult practices and other attempts to foretell the future. Rather, they must listen to the voice of prophecy, and expect the coming of the great Prophet.

Day 3
Jeremiah 1:4–9. The Word of God came as a gift. But (Jeremiah 15:15–19) the prophet himself rejoices in the Word and must accept the moral demands of being the Lord's mouthpiece. (See the NKJV.)

Day 4
Jeremiah 23:18–22. The true prophet (unlike the false one) has 'stood in the council of the Lord', i.e. has spent time in his presence and (Jeremiah 42:1–7) waited patiently for his Word (cf. Habakkuk 2:1).

Day 5
Joel 2:28–29; Micah 3:8. The Spirit of the Lord is the inspirer of prophecy. Cf. 2 Samuel 23:1–4; 2 Peter 1:21.

Day 6
Zechariah 1:2–6. The Word of God outlasts the prophet who spoke it, and possesses life and power in its own right to accomplish that of which it speaks. Cf. Isaiah 55:8–11.

Day 7
Isaiah 59:21. Isaiah predicted the Lord Jesus as endowed with the Spirit and the Word – and envisaged Jesus' people as people of the Word. Cf. Isaiah 42:1–4 ('justice', literally 'judgment', refers to the truth the Lord reveals); 61:1–2.

Questions

1. How can the story of Hosea encourage us if we find ourselves living through testing circumstances, even perhaps, an unhappy marriage? What difference would there be in the way we view those difficulties?
2. If the Word of God outlasts the prophet who spoke it (see number 6 above), what is the lasting legacy for today of the prophets outlined in this chapter?

Who and when, but above all, why and what

So, after, all, the prophets were just folk like us, needing forgiveness (Isaiah), all too aware of their disabilities (Jeremiah), facing up to the call of God (Amos), learning of him and his ways in the knocks and buffetings of life (Hosea), and needing the nourishment of his Word (Ezekiel). But what about the rest of the prophets and their books? How are we to understand and tackle them? We can make a useful start by glancing at Judges 6 – 8.

Judges 6 – 8 is one of many great stories in the book of Judges. The situation was dire. Hordes, led by Midian, were turning the land of Israel into a desert, and reducing daily life to miserable subsistence (6:2–5), but they proved no match for Gideon, the man whom God called (6:11–14), and his army of 300 men (7:1–7). What a story! God's work done in God's way receives God's blessing. But that is only the outer shell of history. In reality, Midian was not the problem and Gideon was not the solution. The problem (6:1) was 'doing evil in the eyes of the Lord'. In other words, they fell out of the power of the Lord before they fell into the power of Midian. The essence of this 'doing evil' was 'you have not listened' (6:10). The Lord's people had committed the cardinal sin of deserting the Word of God (cf. Amos 2:4). Consequently, the Lord's first move was not to send Gideon, the deliverer, but to send a prophet (Judges 6:7).

And that is, in a nutshell, what the prophets are all about. The Lord's people possess the Lord's Word. Their first calling is to hear and obey. Their greatest sin is to fail to listen. Their first need always is to be called back to the Word.

Moses

Even though Abraham is called a prophet (Genesis 20:7), the great line of Old Testament prophets began with and stemmed from Moses. He is the standard by which all prophets are to be tested (Deuteronomy 34:10). As with all the prophets, his ministry was to declare God's truth, and call his people to face up to a life of obedience to the revealed Word of God (e.g. Deuteronomy 30:11–20). He also predicted the coming of the 'prophet like Moses' (Deuteronomy 18:15–22). In effect this meant that every next prophet was seen in the light of this expectation: is this the great, promised prophet like Moses? This expectation was still alive at the time of the last prophet, John the Baptist (John 1:19–21).

Samuel

We do not know how many unnamed prophets there were, like the one in Judges 6:8 (e.g. 1 Kings 13:1, 11). 'Bands' and 'schools' of prophets existed (e.g. 1 Samuel 10:5; 19:20; 2 Kings 2:3, 5, 7; 6:1), but the prophetic movement as such was lifted out of a period of decline (1 Samuel 3:1) by the call of Samuel, and the revelation of the Word of the Lord to him (1 Samuel 3:7, 19 – 4:1). We do not have a detailed account of Samuel's prophetic ministry, but 1 Samuel 7:3–6 and 12:6–25 show that he sounded the typical notes of repentance, returning to the Lord, and bringing life under the Word of God. We see this in action, for example in 1 Samuel 7:6 where Samuel plays his part as the last of the 'judges' (cf. 1 Samuel 12:11), 'putting people's lives to rights' (which is what 'judging' means). One aspect of the ministry of a prophet is brought strongly to the fore in Samuel: the prophet as a man of prayer. This accords with the first reference to a prophet in Genesis 20:7 and reappears explicitly in the ministry of Jeremiah (e.g. Jeremiah 11:14; 14:11). In the history of Samuel, the gift, the Word he was to speak, is linked with the place of prayer (1 Samuel 8:6–7; 15:11, 16, 21–22). His national ministry began (7:5) and ended (12:23) in prayer. Prayer was the way of victory (7:9). Alike in disappointment (8:6), perplexity (8:21) and rage (15:11), he turned to prayer. Being a prophet then was in no way the automatic or mechanical exercise of a 'gift': turn on the tap and the revelation came. It was part of the life of disciplined spirituality and communing with God.

Jeremiah calls this 'standing in the council of the Lord' (23:18, 21–22). The word *sôd* means 'council', a gathered group, in Psalm 89:7, of God's 'holy ones'. In this way it indicates that the prophet becomes party, so to speak, to the heavenly consultation where decisions are taken (cf. 1 Kings 22:19–22). He is made 'wise before the event'. But *sôd* is also 'counsel' and 'fellowship' (Psalm 55:14), and in Job 19:19 'my intimate friends' is literally, 'men of my counsel/fellowship'. A prophet was someone brought intimately close to the Lord, and this meant repentance, standing before the Lord (cf. 1 Kings 17:1), and (as NKJV) 'taking out the precious from the vile' (Jeremiah 15:19).

Elijah and Elisha

Deuteronomy 13 tackles head on the problem of false prophecy. It outlines the case of a prophet who is able to offer 'credentials' in the form of signs and wonders to validate his ministry. To Moses, this is nothing like enough. 'Don't take the lead from his signs,' he says in effect. 'Examine his doctrine. Is he trying to lead the people away from the God who is known in Israel (verse 2), the Lord, their redeemer and deliverer from Egypt (verses 5, 10)? Is he true to established revelation?'

This aspect of the work of the prophet is central to the ministry of Elijah and Elisha (1 Kings 17 – 2 Kings 13). The prophets were not innovators but essentially custodians, trustees, conservators of the deposit laid down by Moses. Their task was to call the people to the Lord and hold them there, not to say 'Move on', but 'Come back' (cf. 2 John 9). Elijah and Elisha lived at a time (c. 850–800 BC) when Baalism had gone beyond being a novel way of worshipping the Lord, and was threatening to become a replacement (1 Kings 16:31–33; 18:21; 19:10; 2 Kings 1:3). It was the task of these two prophets to utter a resounding 'No.' They had the prophetic task of repudiating error, reiterating sound doctrine, and re-establishing sound practice.

Since we cannot dwell on their whole ministry, we will take Elijah's resolute action on Mount Carmel as a case in point. Please read 1 Kings 18:20–40.

Elijah was a monotheist

He was, of course, concerned that his people should choose correctly which God they served, and which God should have pride of place in Israel. Therefore part of his prayer (1 Kings 18:36) was that the Lord would establish his claim as 'God in Israel', that is, to be in a special sense the God of this people in this locality. This did not mean that he recognized any other 'god', any more than Paul did when he spoke of 'gods many and lords many' (1 Corinthians 8:5–6). Such language was simply evidence of living in a multi-faith environment. His opening demand, however, was that the people should make their decision about who God is, the Lord or Baal (1 Kings 18:21). To this end, Elijah set up a prayer-contest with the prophets of Baal whereby 'the God who answers … he is God' – not 'God in Israel', but absolutely 'God'. This was the outcome, in the unanimous cry of verse 39: 'The LORD, he is God' – again, not 'our God' or 'God in Israel' but the absolute and sole Deity.

Elijah was an exclusivist

Elijah rejected not only Baal, but Baalism in its totality. As we have noted, Baal worship was based on 'sympathetic/imitative magic', to do on earth what you wanted

Baal to do in heaven in the hope that he would be stimulated to imitate. Since the Baal prophets wanted fire from heaven, they had to do their best (though without using fire, which was against the rules of the contest, 1 Kings 18:25) to convey this idea to Baal. Therefore they cut themselves and danced (verses 26, 28), presumably in the hope that the down-flowing blood and the leaping might suggest down-flowing fire and leaping flames. This is imitative magic at work. We see, then, that Elijah's insistence on pouring tank after tank of water (verses 33–35) was more than making things difficult for the Lord, and enhancing the miracle of the fire. It was a visible, total denial of Baalistic magic. If you want fire to fall, the last thing you must do is pour water! That would utterly bewilder poor old Baal. Elijah not only wanted to deny Baal any status as divine; he also wanted to deny the theology of Baal by ruling out any magical element in the worship of the Lord.

Elijah's exclusivism, however, went even further: the eradication of Baal and Baal-worship, as far as possible, from Israel. Therefore the officiants of Baal had to be exterminated (1 Kings 18:40). He did not see Baal and his officers as having a contribution to make to the richness of a multi-faith situation, nor as contributing an insight into the totality of truth. They were a cancer to be cut out. For him, and the prophets, there was no 'live and let live'. They did not accept that any and every religion is true, provided someone believes it. Error is deadly, and Elijah dealt with it in terms suited to his own time and day. In this he set us an example, not of method, but of a conviction, zeal and holy spiritual outrage which we should covet, and find means of expressing within the norms and forms of the present day.

Elijah was a traditionalist

He stood for established truths, and the old paths. Notice, therefore, that within the breakaway northern state, he built an altar with twelve (not ten, cf. 1 Kings 11:29–31) stones, for, like all the prophets, he held to the foundational constitution of the Lord's people (18:31), and insisted that the name 'Israel' belonged to the twelve-tribe totality and not to any secessionist group. In the same spirit, when he prayed, his prayer was addressed to the 'God of Abraham, Isaac and Israel', the God of the fathers.

That was Elijah, and such were all the prophets.

The prophets in place, time and Scripture

It is important to remember that each prophet lived at some particular place and time, and that it is through what he said, relevant to that time and situation, that he speaks to us today.

Dating the prophets is not an easy task, but, taking the word 'approximately' seriously, their 'date-line' would look something like this:

Approx. date	700s	600s	500s	400s	Bible
780	Jon.				2 Kgs 14:25
760	Amos				Amos 1:1 2 Kgs 14:23 – 15:7; 2 Chr. 26
750	Hos.				Hos. 1:1 2 Kgs 14:23 – 15:7; 2 Chr. 26
740	Isa.				Isa. 1:1; 2 Kgs 15:1–7; 15:32 – 16:20; 18:1 – 20:21; 2 Chr. 26 – 32
740	Mic.				Mic. 1:1; 2 Kgs 15:12 – 16:20; 18 – 20; 2 Chr. 27 – 32
640		Nah.			2 Kgs 22 – 23; 2 Chr. 34 – 35
		Zeph.			Zeph. 1:1; 2 Kgs 22 – 23; 2 Chr. 34 – 35
620		Jer.			Jer. 1:2–3; 2 Kgs 22 – 25; 2 Chr. 34 – 36
610		Hab.			2 Kgs 22 – 25; 2 Chr. 34 – 36
600			Dan.		Dan. 1 – 6
580			Obad.		Obad. 10–14; 2 Kgs 25; 2 Chr. 36; Lam.
570			Ezek.		Ezek. 1:1–2; 33:21–22; 2 Kgs 24; 2 Chr. 36
520			Hag.		Hag. 1:1; Ezra 3 – 6
			Zech.		Zech. 1:1; Ezra 3 – 6
430				Mal.	

Jonah is an undated prophecy. The reference in 2 Kings tells us only when his prediction was fulfilled, not when he made it, so we can only approximate him as earlier than the reign of Jeroboam II (786–746 BC) or in the first years of that reign. Dating Hosea after Amos arises from the fact that he reflects a less stable society, the early signs of the collapse of the Northern Kingdom. Nahum, too, and Habakkuk are placed where they are in the timeline more by the contents of their prophecies than necessarily when they themselves lived. Nahum is typically secretive, and none of the prophets advertised themselves. We do not even know where Elkosh (Nahum 1:1) was. Nahum 3:8 suggests that Thebes had fallen (664 BC), but the fall of Nineveh (612 BC) was in the future. As is well known, many specialists think of three Isaiahs: the Isaiah of Jerusalem in the 700s; the 'second Isaiah' in Babylon (c. 550 BC); and the 'third Isaiah' after the return in 539 BC. Likewise, many propose a much later date for Daniel. Joel does not appear at all on our timeline because it is not possible to decide between (say) the eighth and the fifth centuries. There is evidence each way. But the material point for all the prophets is that each lived and worked in a specific historical and social context, and sometimes knowing that context helps us to understand more fully what they wrote.

Speakers to writers

Is it correct to think of any of the prophets as 'writing'? They were preachers, weren't they? Did they also write out their own books?

It has been something of a fashion among specialists to depict the prophets' books as, on the whole, slow growths: the named prophet contributed some sort of core which his disciples recorded, and then proceeded, with attempted fidelity to what their master would have taught, to enlarge the core for the benefit of ongoing generations. The result is therefore an anthology rather than a book. Nowadays there is a greater willingness to see the end product as a coherent whole, rather than a collection of snippets, but the idea of an original core, growing under the hands of a continuing school of thought, tends to remain.

We need to remember that this is entirely suppositional. We know that Isaiah had a group called his 'disciples' (8:16–18). We do not actually know that this was the case with any other prophet. However, it may stand to reason that such groups would have gathered round a master. But, according to Isaiah 8, the task of the group was to preserve and conserve, not to develop and add. Furthermore, is there not something abnormal about a man who is convinced that what he is saying is couched in the very words of God, and who does not then commit it to the safety and stability of a written form? Would the prophets have played Chinese Whispers with the words of God? I think not.

Here then is another, and more realistic, scenario. Much of the material in the books of the prophets, as we have them, falls into manageable sections of twenty or thirty verses. Any preacher would agree that these passages could not be preached in their present form: they are too closely reasoned, and their substantial points are made too succinctly and too quickly for hearers to keep up and register what is being said. They have none of the built-in expansiveness ('padding', if you like) or repetition (saying the same thing in a different way) which give hearers time to identify with what is being said, dwell on it, and take it in. At best, what we have in the books are sermon notes from which the prophet preached, or, more likely, the carefully crafted and revised script which he filed away in his records, and in the case of Isaiah committed to his literary trustees.

Isaiah opens up a further possibility. Isaiah 8:1 sees the prophet writing up something in a public place ('scroll' is rather 'tablet', as ESV), and the same thing happens in 30:8 where 'tablet' translates 'table', a large flat surface, and 'scroll' is the ordinary scrolled book. In the former place, Isaiah is ordered to put up a public advertisement; in the latter, he also makes a private record. Would we say then,

'Hire a hoarding space, and at the same time make a written record for preservation'? And did all the books of the prophets start like that? The answer cannot be 'Yes', for we do not know, but it certainly cannot be 'No', for the same reason. It must be 'Why not?' The prophets were educated men living in a high culture, but above all, were seriously aware that they were vehicles of the Word of God in the words of God.

Forth-telling and foretelling

Ezekiel's task was the task of all: 'speak my words … speak with my words' (2:7; 3:4). The prophets were called and sent to tell out the Word of God. To what extent did they also predict what was yet to happen?

John the Baptist offers us a case in point, as concise as his message. He said, 'Repent, for the kingdom of heaven is near' (Matthew 3:1–2). So the answer is 'Yes'. He did predict the future: it was fully half of his message. But – and this is the key point – his prediction of the future was a message to his contemporaries. It was not given for the sake of prognostication, to draw up a calendar of coming events, but to give force to what he wanted to say in the present. He spoke of the future only so that his contemporaries could take that future into account in their present response. John spoke to his own day, and he used his awareness of the future to give weight and urgency to his message in his own situation. So it was with all the prophets. When future events are heralded, it is not so as to provide an almanac of times to come, but to apply moral pressure of one sort or another to those to whom he was speaking.

A case in point

Those who allocate Isaiah 1 – 55 to two separate prophets do so in part because, to make Isaiah of Jerusalem the author of all of it, would involve him in predicting both the Babylonian exile (which did not happen until a century after his time), and also the return from Babylon (nearly two centuries ahead). It is not so much a matter of questioning such ability to predict so far ahead – that would be like penalizing a man for being good at his job! It is rather a matter of asking what *present* useful function such *remote* predictions would fulfil. Take, for example, the promise of a return from Babylon. Isaiah 40:1 says, 'Comfort my people', but what sort of comfort would it be if Isaiah were saying, 'Don't worry, chaps, it will be all right in 200 years'? Cold comfort, indeed! The picture changes, however, when we note that Isaiah himself says nothing about a century or two centuries ahead. It is our knowledge of history that contributes these two time factors. We cannot even say if Isaiah himself knew anything about the length of time involved. He is silent on the subject. But even though Assyria was the superpower of his day, Babylon was a would-be superpower, and a force to be reckoned with. A prediction of Babylonian exile was a live contemporary possibility, and a valid message to the day. Likewise, the prediction of a sure and certain return would have been a very comforting reassurance, just as the undated but ever-imminent return of the Lord Jesus is to us. This is what we mean by prediction related to moral pressure.

Making a start, getting ahead

As with the rest of the Bible, the major hurdle in the way of understanding the prophets is ignorance. The two questions 'What does the Bible say?' and 'What does the Bible mean?' must be kept separate. Very often, when people say they don't read the Bible because they don't understand it, they are talking about the second question, not the first. Huge areas of the Bible are simply good stories, easy to read, memorable in content – such as Genesis or the whole sweep of books from Joshua to Esther, the four Gospels and the Acts. If people say they don't understand these books, they usually mean that they don't always readily see why bits of them are in the Bible at all, and how they apply today. But they are, in fact, perfectly understandable as stories, and that's where we should start. Get acquainted with what the Bible says and let the answers to other questions come in the course of time as knowledge and experience grows.

It is the same with the prophets. Familiarity breeds understanding. So:

1. Read, read and read again

The Bible is such a wonderful book that, the more thoroughly we know the whole, the more readily we understand the part. Generally speaking, even if on other grounds you happen to be wedded to the Authorized Version of 1611, you will undoubtedly find a more recent version beneficial for the purposes of reading through. The recent English Standard Version, for example, or the New King James Version (the Revised Authorized Version), or the New International Version, or, for absolute beginners, the Good News Bible. Remember, this is to start with, just a getting-to-know-you exercise.

2. Use manageable helps

We all work to a limited budget of time, and nothing is more guaranteed to lead to failure than being too idealistic. Satan loves idealists, because he knows they will set impossible targets, attempt too much, and then give up! Defeat Satan by realism – what can you realistically hope to achieve? To move beyond the sort of reading and re-reading which establishes basic knowledge of the content of the Bible, something like the *New Bible Commentary, 21st Century Edition*, gives brief and easy help, explaining the main difficulties, making the flow of thought clear. The *Crossway Bible Guides* break books up into sensible portions and give very useful help. See also some other suggestions in the book list (p. 205).

3. Ask the right questions

The question 'When?' (When did this prophet live and work?) may sometimes produce illumination, but the questions 'What?' and 'Why?' always will – 'What is he saying, and why is he saying it?' The prophets present reasoned and well-argued material, and sentences beginning 'for/because' (the NIV is very weak here) are extremely important. They bring us into the situation the prophet is addressing – a situation, incidentally, which is more often than not amazingly identical to ours The equally important question 'What?' can be tackled by writing out the passage in our own words, or just making sure that we are grasping the facts, the sequence in which they occur, and the thrust of the prophet's argument. But again, remember, don't tackle too much at a time. Keep it manageable. The principle behind all this is that, what the prophet was saying then, he is still saying today, and his message to them is his message to us. It is the question 'What?' which brings us face to face with 'the word of our God' which 'stands for ever' (Isaiah 40:8).

Spending a week with Haggai

If you are not familiar with the books of the prophets, Haggai is a straightforward place to start. The Babylonians had sacked Jerusalem in 586 BC and taken Judah into exile in Mesopotamia (where Israel had been since 722 BC when Samaria fell to the Assyrians). Cyrus the Persian conquered Babylon in 539 BC and began a policy of repatriation. Ezra 3 records how the returnees made a start on temple building, but the work stalled (Ezra 4). From 520 onwards, Haggai and his fellow prophet Zechariah (Ezra 5:1) led a movement to build the house of the Lord.

Read through Haggai, over and over again, using this outline:

1. Two messages on the same day: the ill consequences of leaving the house of the Lord unbuilt (1:1–11).
   ▶ To Zerubbabel and Joshua (1:1–2).
   ▶ To the people: the neglected house: the cause of their ills (1:3–11).
   (Two 'calls' to 'give careful thought'.)

2. The first 'I am with you' message (1:12–15a).
3. The second 'I am with you' message (1:15b – 2:9).
4. Two messages on the same day: the blessed consequences of building the house (2:10–23).
   ▶ To the people: the rebuilt house, cause of bless-
     ing (2:10–19).
   (Two 'calls' to 'give careful thought'.)
   ▶ To Zerubbabel: the restoration of David's house
     (2:20–23).

See how carefully Haggai has edited his ministry into a
balanced presentation. He used 2 Samuel 7:1–11 as a tem-
plate, starting with a plan to build the Lord's house, and
ending with the Lord's promise to build David's house.
The Lord promised that he would live in his house, at the
heart of his people. The 'house' is a pledge of the
indwelling of the Lord. To leave the house unbuilt meant
that it was a matter of indifference to them whether the
Lord was among them or not.

When the Lord appoints the means of enjoying his presence, he expects us to make use of them. For example, the
public means of enjoying his presence: worship, the
Lord's Supper, Christian fellowship; the private means of
enjoying his presence: prayer and Bible reading. To neg-
lect these signifies it is a matter of indifference to us
whether the Lord is with us or not.

Question

Take some time to select a prophet and grapple with the
'what? and why?' questions (what is he saying and why is
he saying it?). What insight have you gained into God's
message for his day, and God's message for us today?

14

All this – and wisdom too!

So, yes, the Old Testament is a real treasure trove, full of good stories and rich teaching, revealing the Lord God in his majesty as Creator, his grace as Saviour, his power as Deliverer, his constancy in mercy and forbearance and his faithfulness to his Word. History, poetry and prophecy combine in a rounded revelation of the Lord, and of his will for his people, both in the present and in the coming glory. But the Old Testament also reveals what it calls 'wisdom', the principles and practices of applying truth to life, so as to make right decisions and live the wise life, the life that pleases God, trusting what he says about himself.

Wisdom in six verses

Proverbs 1:2–7, a preface to the whole book, is a rich collection of the main words of the wisdom vocabulary.

▶ Verse 2. 'Wisdom' (*ḥokmâ*) combines knowing the truth with knowing how to apply the truth to life. 'Discipline' (*mûsār*) is setting the right direction for life, and holding on course. 'Understanding' and 'insight' (the verb *bîn*, and the noun *bînâ*) stress 'discernment', seeing to the heart of a matter.

▶ Verse 3. 'Prudent' (verb *śākal*) includes 'success' (cf. 'successful', Joshua 1:8), the sort of carefully thought-out action that achieves its goal. 'Right' (*ṣedeq*, 'righteousness') means acting according to the true standard or norm – God's revealed norm, of course; 'just' (*mišpaṭ*) is often used of the 'authoritative decisions' the Lord has made (and revealed for our obedience). Here it can therefore mean acting according to God's revealed wisdom, or it can simply call for making correct decisions in any given case. 'Fair' (*mêsārîm*) is as much 'straightforward uprightness' as 'equity' (NKJV, ESV), 'honest' as much as 'fair'.

▶ Verse 4. 'Prudence' (*'ormâ*) is 'shrewdness' in the best sense, but the related adjective (*ārûm*) in Genesis 3:1, though used there in the bad sense of 'crafty', points to carefully planned action in facing a situation so as to get results. 'Simple' is 'gullible' through lack of thought-out basic principles, therefore easily led astray, and, in that sense, 'weak'. 'Discretion' (*mĕzimmâ*) is translated as an adjective, 'crafty', in Proverbs 12:2, and as 'purpose(s)' in Jeremiah 30:24; 51:11. It calls for a planned, thoughtful approach to life, the opposite of allowing the haphazard flow of events to take over, but rather imposing our own considered pattern on the way we live.

▶ Verse 5. 'Listen' is an important word: to listen to the Word of God so as to obey it. Wisdom (2:6) is the Lord's gift, but he conveys it by speaking ('from his mouth'), and we receive it (2:2) by 'turning our ear' to what he says. 'Learning' is *leqaḥ*, from the verb *lāqaḥ*, 'to take, take possession, take hold of'. Hence the idea here is not that of adding to learning, as NIV, but firming up one's grasp of the truth. 'Guidance' (*taḥbûlôṯ*) may be related to *heḇel*, 'rope', *ḥōḇēl*, 'sailor', 'ship's captain', in which case it refers to 'steering a correct course'; or, if it is related to the verb *ḥāḇal*, 'to unite, make a bond', then it is the activity of 'putting two and two together', having a right understanding of things as they are, how they are related, how they 'work', and where they are going.

▶ Verse 6. 'Understanding' is 'discerning, seeing to the

heart of'. 'Proverbs' (*māšāl*) means a pithy way of putting things, whether in a short saying (e.g. Ezekiel 19:3), or making an example of someone (Ezekiel 14:8), or even a longer poem, in Isaiah 14:4, a 'taunt'. 'Parable' (*mĕlîṣâ*) from *lûṣ*, to mock or scorn; it is a derisive exposure. 'Riddles' are not intended to baffle, but to provoke thought, to pose a problem so as to lead to the answer, as in Samson's 'riddle' (Judges 14:12).

► Verse 7. The 'fear of the Lord' is the only context in which true wisdom can be found, grasped and increased. Far from distorting it, or forcing it into an alien grid, biblical spirituality, hearing the Word of God, walking with God, guarantees truth. Outside this, our best efforts result in 'folly'. The word here is *'ĕwîl*, the 'fathead', always confident he is right, unteachable, but forever getting it wrong (Proverbs 10:21; 12:15; 27:22; etc.). He is close partner to the *kĕsîl*, the 'thickhead', equally unteachable and opinionated (e.g 1:22; 14:16; 17:10; 26:4–5). In the Bible we also meet the *nābāl*, the person without a controlling sense of moral values or responsibilities (e.g. 1 Samuel 25:25; Job 2:10; Psalm 53:1).

Basically, then, wisdom is the accurate application of truth to life. Life presents us with conundrums and challenges of all sorts. Everything in us wants, over and over, to ask the question 'Why?' But as we speedily discover, another question also presses: 'How do I tackle this situation, live through this trial?' Or, on a less critical level, for the daily round and common task, 'Is this practice or that, this proposal or that, allowable?' Such questions map out the habitat of biblical wisdom.

Proverbs: to know wisdom

When Moses set up leaders in Israel (Deuteronomy 1:9–18), extending from the oversight of groups of a thou-

sand down to groups of ten, we naturally think of a legal
system, higher and lower courts, and the settlement of
cases at law. This was, of course, part of the plan, but, as
Exodus 18:20 puts it, the intention was essentially wider:
to 'show them the way to live'. 'Law' was broader than
legislation; it was all the 'teaching' the Lord granted by
revelation through his chosen agents. The leaders of thousands, hundreds, fifties and tens were in principle there to
apply the Lord's truth to life. Israel was called to walk in
the way of divine wisdom.

Some people were specially gifted in seeing to the heart
of a matter (cf. Judges 9:7–21; 1 Samuel 14:2–21; 2 Samuel
20:15–22), and verses like Jeremiah 18:18 (cf. Proverbs
24:23) suggest that 'the wise' exercised a recognized ministry alongside prophet and priest. Solomon was the foremost 'wise man', and to a unique degree the fount of
Israel's wisdom (1 Kings 4:29–34). It was natural, therefore, for such a collection as the book of Proverbs to be
brought under Solomon's wing (Proverbs 1:1), not
because he was the author of the whole book (cf. 30:1;
31:1), but because Solomon's wisdom was the norm, and
his name was the validation everyone recognized. Yet
when, of course, Proverbs 10:1; 25:1 attribute authorship
to Solomon, there is no reason to doubt that we are listening to the uniquely wise king.

Reading Proverbs

1. Proverbs requires slow and meditative reading
Even when verses obviously belong together in a connected presentation (e.g. 24:30–34 on the lazybones;
31:10–31 on the good wife), pretty well each verse offers a
thought to be pondered. The same is true where each
verse is a separate 'saying', though we need to be careful,
for even with seemingly random sayings it is always
worthwhile to be alert to possible interconnections.
Proverbs 28, for example, seems at first sight just one thing
after another, but see how it opens and closes on the
theme of the wicked, the righteous and the poor (verses

1–3, 27–28). Verses 4–9 deal broadly with forsaking or keeping the law. There are other connections as well, all circling round the central truth of verses 13–14. It must never simply be presumed that any given verse has no relationship to its context. Thoughtful pondering of each verse is the order of the day for reading Proverbs.

2. Proverbs 1 – 9
This passage is the longest connected statement in the book and a good summary of its leading ideas. Read it through with the following running outline in mind:

1. Introduction (1:1–9).
   ▶ The purpose of the book (verses 2–6).
   ▶ The basic principle and the basic exhortation (verses 7–9).
2. The two voices (1:10–33).
3. Wisdom versus sexual aberration (2:1–22).
4. The good life: within God's will (3:1–35).
5. Three priorities (4:1–27).
6. Sexual morality (5:1–23).
7. Three defects (6:1–19).
8. The good life under threat (6:20–35).
9. The call of the harlot and the call of wisdom (7:1 – 8:36).
10. The two voices (9:1–18).

This is, of course, only a running outline. Proverbs is too rich, too allusive to be straitjacketed, but so many leading themes are announced here that the chapters are a micro-cosm of the world as Wisdom sees it. No secret is made of the awful perils of sexual misconduct (or of the true delights of marriage, 5:15–20). Above all, Wisdom sees life as choices. This is why the whole passage is bracketed by the two competing voices: the clamour of Folly and the attractive invitation of Wisdom. Life is listening, and everything is finally decided by which voice we choose to hear. On the one hand there is a voice of seduction, rich in promised delights, but to listen to that voice is to sign one's own death warrant (7:21–27). The voice of Wisdom is, in retrospect, the voice of Jesus, for we cannot read 8:22–31 without being drawn into the depths of Colossians 1:15–17, and worshipping him who for us is wisdom from God (1 Corinthians 1:30).

3. Keep aware of the bedrock

Think of an area like Dartmoor with all its hundreds of square miles of farmland, pasturage and wilderness. It is liberally scattered with granite, often just stones, rocks and chippings, but every now and again huge outcrops called tors, capped with enormous granite shapes. But what we see as bits of granite and upthrustings of granite is actually the ever-present bedrock of the moor. It is there all the time even though we only become aware of it here and there. So it is with Proverbs.

'God' and 'the Lord'

Here are some statistics: 'God' is referred to five times. For example, Proverbs 2:16–19 is about the 'wayward' woman, her seductive attractions (verse 16) and the mortal peril of consorting with her (verses 18–19). 'Right,' we might say, 'the warning is always timely, even though we are already all too aware of the deadliness of sexually transmitted diseases.' But that is not the point. The deadliness of associating with her is that she has 'ignored the covenant she made before God' (verse 17). That's the real peril: to link with what is actively, wilfully, anti-God. Note the contrasting tones of 3:3–4.

Likewise, Yahweh, 'the LORD', is referred to over eighty times, and in exactly the same way. To ignore the call of Wisdom is serious because it is in fact choosing not to fear the Lord (Proverbs 1:29). A man may slip off for a secret rendezvous with an adulteress, but the Lord is observing (5:20–21; cf. 15:3), and sees even the heart (16:5). There are examples on every page, but the point is obvious: the voice of Wisdom is the voice of the Lord, and to heed the Word of God and obey is the way of Wisdom. Many commentaries note similarities and identities between Israel's wisdom literature and that of pagan nations, as if Proverbs were no more than secular advice, the product of human thought at its best. Not so! Under this whole landscape of Proverbs is the bedrock of the unchanging God, the Lord, who lets his name be heard every so often just to prove the point. The foundation of all true Wisdom is reverence for him; the way of Wisdom is listening to what he says.

Ecclesiastes: Does Wisdom make any difference?

The author of Ecclesiastes calls himself Qoheleth (1:1 NIV, 'Teacher', more commonly 'Preacher', NKJV, ESV). The use of the definite article in Ecclesiastes 7:27 (*haqqohelet*, 'the Qoheleth') suggests that it is meant to be a function rather than, or as much as, a personal name. He is 'the Convenor', calling an audience together to hear what he has to say.

It is understandable that commentators speak of Qoheleth as a pessimist. After all, he does say that 'everything is meaningless' (e.g. 1:2). All of life is like chasing the wind (1:14; 2:17), whether pleasure (2:1), achievement (2:11) or even wisdom (2:15). He professes to hate life (2:18). Work gets you nowhere (3:9). The gross national product disappears into ever grosser appetites (5:11). Far too often the wealthy lack the ability to enjoy their wealth (6:1–2). Since every page offers this sort of material, we might well say, 'Surely a pessimist indeed!'

Alongside this, however, the authentic voice of Wisdom speaks (e.g. 4:5, 8–12; 7:5–12; 9:17 – 10:3; etc.), and there is someone else, usually called the 'pious editor' (e.g. 3:17; 8:2–6, 11–13) who adds in his own 'improving' observations. The result is the mix and match that we call Ecclesiastes! Must we therefore follow those who advocate a theory of multiple authorship: a core of unacceptable pessimism and cynicism which other writers undertook to 'correct' or make acceptable by adding in orthodox bits and inserting helpful devotional pieties?

Well, to be frank, if you believe that, you will believe anything! Supposing we were to find a book of undiluted pessimism, discordant with the buoyant, expectant faith of the Old Testament, incompatible with the biblical doctrine of the good Creator – would we take steps to promote its publication among the Lord's people? And if, *per impossibile*, we did want it published, would we think we had improved the situation by adding in orthodox bits which contradict both their context and the thrust of the whole book? And that this should be done not once (by the 'wisdom' editor), but twice (through the work of the 'pious' editor)!

Maybe we should start again. First, realism is not pessimism. Any open-eyed person, frankly facing life as it is, has to acknowledge that the world appears to be going nowhere (1:3–10); that pleasure (2:1–3), enterprise and acquisitiveness (2:4–11) add up to nothing; that professor and profligate, prudent and fool die in the same way, and sink into oblivion (2:12–16). People wear themselves out for their bank balance, and to what end (4:8)? Political ambition (4:13–16), unfairness and the rat race (4:8–9), goods without happiness (6:1–6), true worth unacknowledged (9:13–16). To put all this on paper is not to be pessimistic but to be realistic. Life is like that!

If, however, we are to be truly realistic, then alongside this assessment of life, the same cool head must put another set of facts and values. Two realisms lie side by side in 8:12–13. A sinner 'lives a long time', according to verse 12, but, according to verse 13, 'their days will not lengthen'. This sort of thing is of course taken by some as justification for the view that later editors 'put in their spoke'. But we must ask again, would any sane person think he was improving a book by contradicting it? We have no right to assume lunacy in ancient editors! 'It is surely', says Michael Eaton (see the book list, p. 205), 'more likely that juxtaposed contradictions are calculated to draw our attention to the viewpoint of faith in contrast to that of observation. As a point of … observation, there are those who do evil and live long. As a point of faith,

[Qoheleth] holds that this does not go on for ever: he shall not prolong his days.' Eaton notes the contrast between (8:9) 'I saw' (i.e. what things look like), and 'I know' (8:12), the voice of conviction. 'Why', he asks, 'should we postulate a clumsy self-contradicting scribe? Why may not [Qoheleth] reply from the viewpoint of faith?'

Wisdom makes all the difference

Of course Wisdom makes no difference. How could it? For the wise and the fool alike 'all streams flow into the sea, yet the sea is never full' (Ecclesiastes 1:7). The world we see is repetitive, constant and enigmatic. Life is frustrating, unpredictable, unfair, delightful and disappointing all at once – all the things the realistic Qoheleth observed. Wisdom makes no difference. For a person, however wise, however versed in God's revealed truth, the world is just the same as for those Qoheleth sees as fatheads, thickheads and without moral sensitivity.

And yet Wisdom makes all the difference.

> Heaven above is softer blue;
> Earth around is sweeter green;
> Something lives in every hue
> Christless eyes have never seen.

So wrote G. W. Robinson in his hymn, 'Loved with Everlasting Love', and C. S. Lewis expressed it inimitably in his profound allegory, *Till We have Faces*. Qoheleth, a realist in faith as much as in observation, would totally agree. This is why that other equally realistic voice, the voice of divine Wisdom, speaks insistently, unheralded, throughout his hard-nosed review of life as it confronts us. There is always another viewpoint, another construction to be put on things, something else to be said, for now that 'all has been heard, here is the conclusion of the matter: Fear God and keep his commandments ...' (Ecclesiastes 12:13–14).

We might even say that the seemingly erratic arrangement of Ecclesiastes is itself a parable of the truth it has to share. Throughout the book, and without warning, we find that we have moved into a different world, the world of divine truths and directives. Notice, for example, how chapter 7 breaks in on chapter 6. In 6:1, 12 the words 'under the sun' form a bracket round yet another description of the life that is 'meaningless' (6:2, 4, 9, 12): to the observer's eye, life doesn't 'add up' But in 7:1–10 we are in the world of the book of Proverbs, the world of God's Wisdom. It is as if the 'untamed disorder' of the book itself is saying that in the thick of all the unanswered questions, difficulties, enigmas, conundrums of life, the Word of God is also there, and we must ever turn to it and let it bring our distracted thoughts back on course.

Job: wisdom and fellowship with God

The simplest way to discover the book of Job is to start at the end! Job had fallen into sorrow and suffering (Job 1 – 2), and three friends came to console him (2:11–13) (ultimately adding to his grief). Each of them takes it in turn to reply to Job (Job 3 – 25), and, after Job's long (and pretty marvellous) final speech (Job 26 – 31), a character named Elihu (Job 32 – 37) makes his contribution. But at last (Job 38 – 41) the Lord himself breaks the silence.

The Lord says much, but explains nothing. Right to the end, Job's suffering remains a mystery. We are not told why the Lord directed Satan's attention to Job (1:8) in the first place, or why he opened the door to additional trials (2:3–6). The Lord is working in accordance with his own undeclared designs. He does not 'explain', but he does point to himself:

▶ Chapters 38 – 39 exemplify *the wisdom of God*, specially the wisdom that orders all things throughout the physical (38:2–38) and animal (38:39 – 39:30) worlds, the wisdom that always outstrips the human capacity to explain or understand. It is not that these things individually will never be understood, but that there is always that which baffles the human mind. The increasing perimeter of knowledge only increases the perimeter where knowledge meets ignorance, hesitation and hypothesis.

▶ Job 40:1–14 turns to *the justice of God*, and does so in a manner typical of wisdom writing. Job is invited to take God's place on the throne. Has he the power to exercise rule (verse 9)? Has he the moral judgment to discern wickedness and punish it appropriately (verses 10–13)? In other words, would he be able to exercise a just rule? Has he the moral discernment to recognize what true justice should do?

▶ Finally, Job 40:15–24; 41:1–34 bring us face to face with *the power of God*. Two poems of great literary power respectively introduce 'Behemoth' and 'Leviathan'. 'Behemoth' is the plural of the noun *bĕhēmâ*, a 'beast', or as a collective noun, 'animals/cattle'. The plural is a plural of majesty or amplification, '*the* beast *par excellence*'. Leviathan (*liwyātān*) apears in Psalm 104:26 as a sea-monster, in Psalm 74:14 as the hostile 'spirit' of the Red Sea, overcome by the Lord when he divided the Sea and led his people safely through. In Isaiah 27:1 Leviathan stands for the Lord's ultimate enemy, the Serpent, defeated in order to bring his people into their vineyard-inheritance (verses 2–6). Together, Behemoth and Leviathan exemplify the Hebrew idiom of totality expressed by means of contrast: the (*physical*) monster on the *land* and the (*supernatural*) monster in the *sea*. Together in this way they constitute a complete picture of every sort of power: earthly, cosmic, heavenly, beyond anything humankind possesses, but well within the power of God (Job 40:19). 'His Maker can approach him' (NKJV inserts an interpretative 'Only'), and (41:10) 'Who, then, is able to stand against me?'

Not logic but faith

In brief, that is all the Lord said in his long speeches: he is the God of wisdom, justice and power. Now, as soon as we deny any one of these, the world in all its oddity, complexity and unexpectedness, becomes spuriously logical.

► Suppose we say he is wise and just, but lacking in power, every problem of life fits into that gap, for his wisdom and justice have been frustrated by a lack of power to put them into practice.

► Suppose we say he is wise and powerful, but not always just, or just and powerful, but not always wise. Again the world is no longer mysterious. Its inequalities are simply due to a failure in justice, or lack the wisdom that puts things right.

► But proclaim a God who is always wise, always just and always powerful, and there is no longer any escape hatch, no way that our logic will ever make sense of the world we live in. It is, as Ecclesiastes says, 'Vanity' (NKJV), 'Meaningless' (NIV), or as we might put it, it just doesn't add up.

This is what baffled Job's friends and put Job beyond their comprehension. They said the problems of the world have a simple explanation: sin brings calamity and calamity comes from preceding sin. Job replied (with truth, as 1:8; 2:3 prove), 'But not in my case.' They said, 'The world is subject to our logical understanding of it.' Job replied, 'But I don't fall within the scope of your logic. It doesn't work in my case.' And neither it did – nor indeed, as we all know only too well, can it be seen to work in the manifold miseries that make up world experience, past and present.

The interesting thing, and the heart of the meaning of the book of Job, is that in all this the Lord said nothing to Job that he did not know and believe already. Job would have agreed completely with Elihu about the Lord's power, justice and righteousness (37:23). In the deeply moving chapter 28 he noted how human ingenuity can fathom out all sorts of hidden things, but 'where can wisdom be found?' (verse 12). Mankind can find the silver-mine (verse 1). Is there not somewhere a 'wisdom-mine'? 'Where ... does wisdom come from?' (verse 20). Answer: 'God understands the way to it, and he alone knows where it dwells' (verse 23). But Job's credal faith that the Lord possesses all wisdom, justice and power was no help to him as long it was merely a creed.

Everything changed when the Lord himself came and spoke personally and said so. At that point, knowing about God suddenly became knowing God, and faith was restfully content to trust the all-wise, all-powerful, all-just God whose thoughts are not our thoughts, nor are our ways his ways (Isaiah 55:8). Faith, not explanation, is the clue to life – faith, not as credulity, nor as a vague (optimistic) intuition that somehow everything will add up to something, but faith in the Word that the Lord himself speaks, faith in the Lord as he reveals himself.

History: his hidden hand

Two other Old Testament books must be mentioned, though sadly, only with a brevity that mocks their importance.

The book of Esther records an episode in the history of the Judean community in the Persian empire during the reign of Xerxes (486–465 BC), whom the Bible calls Ahasuerus. The 'Judeans' (translated 'Jews' in most versions) are those who elected to stay on in exile after others had taken Cyrus' permission to go home (Ezra 1 – 2). It is clear that they retained unstated priorities and practices (cf. Esther 4:16) which marked them out as a separate, immigrant community, and they attracted the enmity of the king's then favourite, Haman, who plotted genocide. By an extraordinary set of changes, chances and coincidences, the plot was reversed, and it was not Mordecai, a leading Judean, but Haman himself who ended on the gallows!

It all began with a royal 'domestic incident' in which Queen Vashti lost her throne. A beauty contest was organized to select a successor (Esther 1 – 2), and Mordecai's niece, Esther, was thus chosen as 'Miss Persia', and became Queen Esther. Mordecai uncovered a plot against the king, but went unrewarded (2:19–23). When the date for the genocide was announced, he alerted Esther: was it for this she had come to the throne (4:14)? Esther literally took her life into her own hands and approached the king about the genocide plot. Haman's fall from grace was as dramatic as his rise had been swift, and he was replaced by Mordecai (7:1–10)

These are only the bones of a great narrative, but they give us enough background to marvel that there is no mention whatever of God by name, title or implication. Yet he is there, and not as an onlooker, or even as a master chess-player who always has a move at the ready to counter what his opponent does, but as the foreseeing, planning, provident, sovereign mastermind, the God who is 'over all and through all and in all' (Ephesians 4:6). The book of Esther is what Proverbs says 'writ large'.

▶ The story in Esther begins with a number of royal whims (chapters 1 – 2). Proverbs says, 'The king's heart is in the hand of the LORD; he directs it like a watercourse wherever he pleases' (21:1).

▶ At a key moment, what we call 'undesigned coincidences' changed everything (Esther 6:1–10). Proverbs says, 'The lot is cast into the lap, but its every decision is from the LORD' (16:33).

▶ In other words, Esther is not just a fascinating tale of long ago. It exemplifies the way biblical Wisdom understands all history. Behind every event, however unwelcome, however 'incidental', however beneficial, there is the hand and mind of the sovereign Lord of History. History is not only his story, it is his handiwork.

Sadly, Esther also illustrates what happens when the voice of divine Wisdom is ignored and human wisdom takes over. It ends with two chapters of gruesome vengefulness (chapters 8 – 9), whereby we cry out, 'What a response to the delivering hand of God!' And how much better it would have been to live by the directives of Wisdom (Proverbs 25:21–22), leaving it to the Lord to see to his people's continuing safety and their reward, and to apportion and inflict any vengeance that may have been due.

Marriage: his wise and delightful plan

Yes, this is a good place to recall that the Song of Songs is part of our Bible. Even if it is not commonly included in the Wisdom literature (any more than is Esther), yet it is best approached as Wisdom's elaboration of a number of scattered proverbs extolling marriage (e.g. Proverbs 5:15–20) and warning against sexual laxity (e.g. Proverbs 7). In any case, this is how the Song should be approached in the first instance. Read it in one sitting as the parable of 'Solomon' (šĕlōmōh) and 'the Shulammite' (šûlammît, 6:13). Both the name and the title derive from the verb šālem, 'to be complete, whole, fulfilled, at peace', along with its noun šālôm, 'peace, fulfilment, wholeness'. Biblically, this is a rounded, threefold 'wholeness': peace with God, peace in society, and the peace of a fulfilled and integrated personality. The Song portrays the masculine, šĕlōmōh, and the feminine, šûlammît, delighting in love and marriage. We are transported back, as it were, to the Eden which sin forfeited (Genesis 2:18–24), and are allowed to see the wonder and ecstasy of true marital enjoyment.

The Song is beautiful as a piece of literature, as well as in its underlying content. It is also realistic, making no secret of the temptations, longings and testings inseparable from committed love. Typically of Hebrew Wisdom writing, it has a diffuseness which defies over-neat analysis. Often (as in Proverbs, Ecclesiastes and Job) one thought seems to borrow from another. Yet for a first read through, look at it like this: A couple deeply in love; the delights and restraints of being engaged (Song 1:1 – 4:6); married at last (4:7 – 5:1); the testings and triumph of married love (5:2 – 8:14).

All through the Christian centuries, the Song has been seen as an allegory of the relationship of love between Christ and his church. Sometimes this approach has been abused (what approach to the Bible hasn't?), and commentators have pretty well snatched at this verse or that, with no regard to its context, in order to bring out some truth about God's love for us and our responsive love for him. But abuse must not be allowed to take away proper use, though some – even most – today would want to insist that the song is only a lyrical appreciation of pure human love. They would point out (rightly) that, in the Bible, it is sexual intercourse that centrally 'constitutes' marriage, and that the Song's uninhibited sexual delight is its intended contribution to Scripture. Further, they would say (and again, rightly) that this is the Song's first testimony to the world today: in a world which prioritizes sex and makes marriage a sub-topic within sex, the Bible, and the Song, insist that we cannot understand sex, its place, function and joy, until we understand what marriage is, the place it holds, and what makes it work.

This is all true, but *because it is true* another dimension is inevitable. *Because the Song is first and foremost a depiction of union in love and marriage, it must also be an allegory of Christ and the church*. The 'join' is seamless, as, indeed, Paul teaches in Ephesians 5:22–33. Marriage is a constant biblical metaphor of the Lord and his people (e.g. Hosea 2:14–23). Spiritual and religious apostasy is like a wife becoming a harlot (e.g. Jeremiah 3:1; Ezekiel 16; 23); the Lord's covenant is like a marriage covenant (e.g. Jeremiah 31:31–33); and the consummation of the saving work of Jesus is the marriage of the Lamb (Revelation 19:4–9). There is therefore nothing surprising, certainly nothing unbiblical, but rather a necessity and inevitability about interpreting the Song as an extended expression of this basic truth, the marriage bond between the Lord and his people.

Far from being an abuse of Scripture, it 'stands to biblical reason' to do so, and we ought to delight in getting it right. Indeed, like all biblical Wisdom, this approach to the Song of Songs is a perfect illustration of the combination of the heavenly and the earthly, the highly spiritual and the downright earthy, the emotionally uplifting and the severely practical, that so wonderfully marks out the Bible from every other book. Indeed, we might go so far as to say that just as we will never understand sex till we understand marriage, so also we will never understand marriage on the human level until we understand the (marriage) union between Christ and his church, and can sing with the hymn-writer John Newton of 'Jesus, my Shepherd, Husband, Friend'.

A dipstick into biblical Wisdom: some Proverbs each day for seven days

Day 1
Proverbs 2:1–6. Wisdom is both a gift (verse 6) and a search (4). It is revealed truth for us to receive and treasure (1), also to submit to and long for (3–4).

Day 2
Proverbs 3:7–12. Life under Wisdom is committed to the Lord (verse 9), and under his blessing (10). It is also a life of the Lord's educative, loving discipline (11–12).

Day 3
Proverbs 5:15–20. Wisdom extols human love: fidelity, marriage and its joys. It warns strictly against sexual straying (7:24–27).

Day 4
Proverbs 10:11, 19–21, 31–32. This is a very prevalent theme in Proverbs – and, indeed, all through the Bible (James 3:2–8): the proper use of the power of speech, its dangers and benefits.

Day 5
Proverbs 16:1, 4, 9, 33; 21:1–2. Here is another leading theme: the Lord rules and controls everything, however hidden and secret, however high and mighty, however seemingly incidental. The Lord rules and reigns.

Day 6
Proverbs 27:23–27. Put this alongside yesterday's insistence on the Lord's sovereign rule. Proverbs, and the Bible, insist that this does not cancel out our responsibility for our own lives. There is a constant commendation for sensible planning, and the wise ordering of our affairs.

Day 7
Proverbs 30:2–6. The wise man rightly has a realistically humble opinion of himself, and knows that there are crowds of unanswered questions, but he holds the Word of God in high esteem, trusts the Lord of the Word, and affirms the completeness, sufficiency and truthfulness of the Word.

Have you enjoyed these bits of Proverbs? The rest of the book is just as enjoyable. Proverbs is a book to read, read and read again – such insight into life, such practical wisdom, and many a laugh along the way!

Questions

1. How does knowing God (rather than just knowing about him) help you handle the topic of suffering (as it did Job)?
2. The question of suffering is a common difficulty for non-Christians as they consider a Christian faith. How would you approach the topic with them? How can you draw on your own experiences (both of suffering and of God)?

PART THREE

Looking back, looking on, looking up

15

So what is the Old Testament saying to us?

Start by remembering that the Old Testament is 'our book'. Not indirectly or by any sleight of hand. Remember too that our greatest dignity is to be like the Lord Jesus Christ, and this includes the way we think: therefore to us, as to him, the Old Testament is the Word of God, and the Scriptures are the book we must have if we are to know him (Luke 24:27) and to talk about him (verses 44–47). It is the Bible, 'Act One', leading into 'Act Two', providing the facts and explanations without which the New Testament would be diminished and largely unexplained. We should accept, then, that the Old Testament speaks to us, and for our part we should commit ourselves in advance to what it is found to say.

1. Begin at the beginning: God the Creator

The first testimony of the Old Testament is of the God who created the cosmos.

▶ The verb 'to create' (*bārā'*) is used throughout the Old Testament, only of what God does. It is his verb. Wherever it occurs, he is either its subject or its implied subject. Outside the Old Testament, in related languages (so the experts say), the same verb is used of human artistic creation. But it is typical of the Bible's careful use of words that this broader application has disappeared, and *bārā'* is only used when the greatness or newness of the product points to God as its cause. The verb does not necessarily mean 'creation out of nothing' (*ex nihilo*), but in the context of Genesis 1:1 it requires that meaning, for the first move of the Creator was to bring into being the material which he would progressively make into the habitable earth.

▶ Staying for a moment with Genesis 1, the basic matter which God created is described as 'formless and empty' (*tōhû wābōhû*, verse 2). Jeremiah uses the same words in 4:23, to describe an earth devoid of light, stability (verse 24) and life (25), and reduced to desert barrenness (26). Here then is the Bible acting as its own dictionary, explaining its own words. Think of a large mass of rock. To the untutored eye, it means nothing. It 'has neither shape nor make', as we say. But let a skilful sculptor go to work, and there emerges the beauty and meaningfulness which his eye could see. So in Genesis 1:2 the meaningless, barren, unstable, dark, lifeless mass awaited the Creator's word and hand, to bring out the meaningful and beautiful world he had built into this unpromising lump of matter, a world full of vegetable, animal and human life which in his eyes was 'good … very good' (Genesis 1:3, 10, 12, 18, 21, 25, 31).

▶ One other thing about Genesis 1. Notice the sparing and careful way the verb 'to create' is used. It marks the absolute beginning of everything (verse 1), the introduction of animate life (21), and the creation of the first human pair (27). The threefold use of the great creation-verb in relation to humankind (27) not only marks out humans as *the* creature *par excellence*, but, notwithstanding the uniqueness of bearing the divine image, still essentially creaturely.

The simplest way to come to grips with what the Old Testament thinks about God the Creator is to look up the verb 'to create' in a concordance. It is soon clear that 'creating' means a lot more than how everything started. At best, that is a quarter of what the Old Testament teaches.

Think, therefore, of a square where each of the sides represents one facet of God's creative power:

▶ The Creator *originates* everything (Genesis 1).

▶ The Creator *maintains* everything in existence. Nothing lives independently of him. Bluntly, if he stopped his work of creatorial maintenance even for a split second, there wouldn't even be nothing! See, for example, Isaiah 42:5, where all the verbs ('created … stretched … spread … gives …') are actually participles, expressing (as the participle in Hebrew does) an unchanging, unvarying state of affairs, an ongoing relationship and activity.

▶ The Creator *controls* all things in their operation. Isaiah 54:16–17 is typical: the craftsman owes his craft and skill to the Creator (16a) – astonishingly, they share the same creative power. The same personal creative act (the personal pronoun, 'I', is emphatic each time it occurs in verse 16) is responsible for 'the destroyer' and his intention to mar and spoil. But, comfortingly, verse 17 assures us that in this world, mastered by the Creator, there is no such thing as 'evil let loose'. Weaponry is not the master, but is kept within the 'thus far and no further' of the same great God.

▶ The Creator *directs* all things to their appointed goal. See Amos 4:13; 9:5–6, for the Creator's dominance and power over creation (cf. Jeremiah 10:12–16). Isaiah, too, is very daring. In relation to the 'forces' that operate in history, he does not hesitate to say that they are but a 'saw' and the Lord is the carpenter, they are but an 'axe' and the Lord is the woodman (Isaiah 10:15). He has been writing here about the Assyrian assault on Jerusalem (verses 5–14). Certainly the king of Assyria had power – he was the then world's superpower – and it was his will to dominate, his imperialism, that drove him against Jerusalem. He was a mighty agent, fully responsible for his wickedness, but he was also a tool in an omnipotent hand. He gave vent to his wicked designs and the Lord executed his moral purposes (cf. Acts 2:23, better in NKJV, ESV). Isaiah hints at another illustration in 37:29: the horse and its rider. All the energy belongs to the horse, all the direction of that energy belongs to the rider. Job 1 – 2 shows that this is true even in the case of Satan. His activities follow divine direction, are exercised by divine permission, and are kept within divine parameters. Or, to move to another area of Old Testament thinking, creation is moving to new creation (Isaiah 65:17–25), not by natural necessity but by the will and work of the Creator. Night and day follow each other only by his covenant faithfulness (Jeremiah 33:19–26). Sun, moon and stars shine, the sea roars, only by his decree; the stars are in place only because he calls them by name, like so many pet dogs, to do his bidding (Isaiah 40:26). That is God the Creator.

2. Sin and salvation

The New Testament simply takes over the Old Testament view of God the Creator (e.g. Mark 13:19; Acts 4:24–28; Colossians 1:16), and, contrary to much popular thinking, the same is true in the matter of salvation. We have already seen that it is wrong to think of the Old Testament as teaching salvation by works, as if grace was a New Testament discovery. A little more exploration, however, will be helpful.

The record of human life in the Garden (Genesis 2 – 3) looks simple, but it is packed full of deep truth. We have already learned that obedience was the key to enjoyment of the Garden, and that this is the relationship between grace and law everywhere in the Bible. But now think of the moment of temptation (Genesis 3), for it opens up the nature of our sinfulness in the same simple and profound way.

It would be easy to think of the Lord God as overreacting when he cursed Satan, humankind and the ground (Genesis 3:14–19), expelling Adam and his wife from the Garden (verses 23–24) – all this just for eating one fruit!

The Lord God, said the serpent (verses 4–5), has forbidden this fruit, not out of good will, to guard you from death – that is only an idle threat! – but out of ill will, to hold you back from fulfilling your proper potential of becoming like gods. Thus the serpent denied the word of God and impugned the character of God. When they fell into sin, therefore, the human pair acquiesced in these two accusations against God: he is not good at heart, but ill-natured, and his word is false and misleading.

The first sin also involved the whole of human nature in revolt against the whole law of God (verse 6). To see the forbidden fruit as good for food and a delight to the eyes, was a revolt of *the human emotions*. Human desire, at that moment, rebelled against God's will. To think of the fruit as 'desirable for gaining wisdom' was a revolt of *the mind*. Human logic would conclude that, since it is the tree of knowledge, it must give knowledge. But divine logic had drawn a different conclusion: it is the tree of knowledge, but its effect is death. Thus *human reason* rebelled against God. And when she 'took and ate' and 'gave to her husband and he ate', the *human will* rebelled against God. Emotions, mind and will comprise the whole of human nature, *and there was no other law in the Garden. Apart from this one prohibition there was complete liberty* (Genesis 2:16–17). Sin is the rebellion of the whole of human nature: mind, emotions and will, against the whole law of God, impugning the character of God, denying the word of God.

This is the seriousness of sin. Sin, of course, has sad, even tragic, consequences and neither the Bible as a whole nor the story of the Garden shies away from the fact that marital disruption (Genesis 3:12, 20), the fracturing of society as it then existed, economic stress (verse 19) and environmental damage (verse 18) are all the result of sin. To tackle these problems is important in its own right, but to do so is not to solve the problem of sin. Sin is an internal collapse of human nature and character. Sin is alienation from God (verse 8), and, more seriously, his alienation from us, and the provocation of his just judgment and well-merited wrath (verse 24).

We need to be very careful at this point: the animal sacrifices of the Old Testament were God's effective provision for atonement and forgiveness. Nowhere does The Old Testament say that they were *pro tem* or inadequate. Through them, the Lord promised the restoration of sinners to his fellowship. And, as the Psalms abundantly show, our Old Testament brothers and sisters in the family of Abraham, the Israel of God, entered into the good of these spiritual blessings there and then. Yet Romans 3:25 speaks of God exercising 'forbearance' in 'passing over sins previously committed' (NKJV), and Hebrews 10:4 says that 'it is impossible for the blood of bulls and goats to take away sins'.

Well, it must be so, must it not? And for this reason: an animal can provide a body without sin – hence the requirement of 'perfection' (e.g. Exodus 12:5). Furthermore, the ritual of sacrifice, particularly the laying on of hands, can give a true picture of the relation of substitution between the offerer and the offering. But what about the interior nature of sin? The animal cannot share human emotions, cannot reason as does the human mind, or, in particular, consent as does the human will. Animal substitution in fact leaves the sinner 'unsubstituted for' at the points of greatest need.

Only a perfect human can stand in for human sinners, bringing human emotions that never revolted, a mind that always bowed to the Word of God, and a sinless will consenting to the rightness of God's death sentence, and also consenting to stand in the sinner's place. In the Old Testament, it took the towering genius of Isaiah to grasp this fully, and to portray for us the Servant of the Lord: truly human, truly divine, sinless and willing to stand in the place of sinners (Isaiah 53, see Chapter 16). The way of salvation in the Old Testament is the same as in the New. In both Testaments, sinners are invited to trust the promises of God, namely, that he provides atonement by means of a substitutionary offering; to lay their hands on the head of the God-given sacrifice, at one and the same time acknowledging their sins and putting them on the One who stood in their place.

3. The church and its life

The distinguishing mark of the people of God is their possession of the Word of God.

▶ This was the hallmark the Lord God stamped on Adam in the Garden: he enjoyed bounty under the Word of God, the law of the tree of knowledge, 'the law of liberty'.

▶ When 'grace found Noah' (the *meaning* but not the *literal translation* of Genesis 6:8), its outward result was obedience to the Word of God – the word of warning about the flood, and the word of salvation about building the ark (6:14–17, 22; 7:5).

▶ Abraham lived under the Word of God, expressed in the broadest terms (Genesis 17:1), and his supreme test was whether he would do what God said (22:2, 18).

▶ Through Moses, the revealed Word multiplied, becoming itemized and all-embracing: the 'decrees' ('statutes', unchangeable edicts) and 'laws' ('judgments', authoritative decisions and directives), as Deuteronomy 4:1, for example, puts it. Moses insisted that the distinctive speciality of his people among all peoples was their possession of, and submission to, this revealed truth (verses 5–8).

▶ Amos began his book with a parade of the surrounding nations (1:2 – 2:3), before homing in on Judah and

Israel (2:4 – 3:8). The charges laid against the nations are crimes against humanity, violations of the voice of conscience. But the charge against Judah is that they 'rejected the law (teaching) of the Lord and have not kept his statutes (unchangeable edicts)'; and against Israel, that they silenced the voice of prophecy (2:11–12).

Thus the people of God possess the Word of God, the Word he imparted through chosen agents, the Word which is his very voice speaking by revelation.

The central Old Testament story is bracketed between Exodus 24:1–8 and Nehemiah 8. The Israel of God, in its normative Old Testament form, is gathered at Sinai to listen while Moses 'took the Book of the Covenant and read it to the people' and 'they responded, "We will do everything the LORD has said; we will obey"' (Exodus 24:7). Our final glimpse of the Israel of God, in the Old Testament, before they enter the long night of waiting for the Messiah, finds them telling 'Ezra the scribe to bring out the Book of the Law of Moses, which the LORD had commanded for Israel … Day after day … Ezra read from the Book of the Law of God' (Nehemiah 8:1, 18).

The people of the Lord are the people of the Book – a truth about which the New Testament is as clear as the Old.

▶ It took its lead from the insistence of the Risen Jesus that he could only be known and preached as he was revealed in the Old Testament Scriptures (Luke 24:25–27, 32, 46–48).

▶ It is evident in the way in which the Acts equates the growth of the number of disciples with the spread of the Word of God, making them two ways of saying the same thing (Acts 6:7; cf. 12:24), and, as we have seen (pp. 15–17 above), it is the topic of Paul's final letter as the apostolic age closed: the true and real church is the company under the Word of God.

The church within the church

At several points in his letter to the Romans Paul draws an important distinction between outward, formal membership of the people of God and inner conviction and commitment – the work of grace in the heart, that marks true membership. The God-given sign of circumcision, he notes, does not convey the reality of which it speaks (Romans 2:28–29; cf. 1 Corinthians 7:19; Galatians 5:6; 6:15). As such, it indicates an outward, card-carrying status, but not necessarily a real membership. Likewise, someone may trace an impeccable descent from Abraham yet not belong to Abraham (Romans 9:6–7; cf. Matthew 3:9). So, on the one hand, there is such a thing as a membership roll, with names and numbers, but on the other hand, there is a real membership, a church within the church, a membership of the heart, which no human eye can see, count or list, known and cherished by God, his 'elect' (cf. Matthew 24:22, 24, 31; Ephesians 1:4; 2 Timothy 2:19; 1 Peter 1:2).

Now notice that Paul (Romans 9) came to this understanding of the church from the Old Testament. We read in Genesis 17:18–21 that Abraham was concerned over his 'natural' son, Ishmael. God, while promising that Ishmael would not be overlooked in divine care, insisted that, not Ishmael but Isaac, the child yet to be born, was the chosen line: in other words, within the family of Abraham, a principle of selection operated, 'not Ishmael but Isaac' (cf. Romans 9:6–13). Isaiah gave this truth its classical expression. In 8:11–22 he draws a distinction between 'this people' and others, including himself, who first appear simply as 'you' (plural). In a time of national nervousness, they are to live only in the fear of the Lord (Isaiah 8:12–13), and to experience the safety he gives, for to them he will be a 'sanctuary', but to the rest he will be (literally) 'a stone of stumbling' (verses 14–15). In verses 16–18 the 'you' company of verse 13 are the Lord's 'disciples' (16), the guardians of 'the testimony' and 'the law'. Speaking for himself (but presumably for his group), Isaiah testifies to his confident 'waiting' for the Lord to act (17ab), and his personal faith (17b). This (18) makes him and his 'family' a 'sign', literally 'signs' (a plural of amplitude, a 'full, complete sign'), clear and complete pointers to the truth, and a 'symbol' (literally 'wonders', i.e. things to make people stop in their tracks and ask questions). In contrast with a general tendency to consult 'the spirits' and the dead (19), true believers run to 'the law and ... the testimony', the only source of light (20), the only alternative to the darkness (22).

In summary, then, there is a company marked by confident reverence, personal faith, expectant hope, and faithful guardianship of and reliance on the revealed Word of God. These are 'the church within the church', the 'blessed company of all faithful (believing) people', as the Book of Common Prayer used to call them, or, as Isaiah says (66:2, 5), those 'who tremble at his Word'.

The law of God in the life of the believer

So then, throughout the Bible, the people of the Lord are the people of the Book. Or, putting it another way, the people of grace are the people of law. Just as grace brought Noah into a transformed life (Genesis 6:8–9) of obedience (6:14; 7:5), so Christians are called to obey in a life of 'well-pleasing' (Colossians 1:9–10), 'under Christ's law' (1 Corinthians 9:21). In Romans 6 Paul uses three parallel titles for Christians: slaves of obedience (verse 16), of righteousness (19), of God (22). Philippians 2:8, 12 adduces the supreme example of the obedient Jesus to call us to obey. Galatians 3:1 says it is a sort of 'bewitchment' that lures us away from obedience. Acts 5:32 says that it is to those who obey him that God gives his Holy Spirit. Is it not for this reason that the Gospels major on the life (and therefore the example) of Jesus, and why the ethical dimensions of the Christian life figure so largely in the Epistles? We are called to lives that 'adorn the doctrine of God our Saviour in all things' (Titus 2:10, NKJV).

Applying Old Testament law

The principle of obedience to God's law then, laid down in the Old Testament, is prolonged into the New. The people of grace are still the people of the law. But how do Old Testament laws apply to New Testament believers? To this there is no simple, one-size-fits-all answer.

(a) We need to be careful about the word 'law', for the New Testament describes all the Old as 'the law' (Matthew 5:17; Luke 10:26). It would be rash to say that some bits of the Bible no longer apply, for we are called to live under the Word of God, not to subject it to our likes and dislikes. For example, the 'law', in the sense of directives for life, covers religious, moral and civic issues. Do we say, then, that since the church and the 'state' are no longer identical, Old Testament directions for ordering public life are a dead letter? 'The word of our God stands for ever' (Isaiah 40:8); Moses 'received living words to pass on to us' (Acts 7:38). Our proper pre-commitment to discover, believe and accept what is written should rather lead us, even when we face the most seemingly remote, bygone, or apparently trivial matters, to say with Joshua: 'What message does my Lord have for his servant?' (Joshua 5:14).

(b) Some elements of the Old Testament are now illustrative and instructive, but not directive. The sacrifices in Leviticus, and great verses like 17:11, teach us vivid lessons about the cross of Christ, but the commands to offer these sacrifices no longer apply. The commands as such underline the divine authority of the truth that the sacrifices embody, but this is now fully and finally realized in Jesus. Earlier we used the illustration of the grain in a piece of wood, and how the end-grain was in fact there from the start but did not emerge in its fullness until the end. So the cross of Calvary was, from the start, the concealed intention of the sacrifices, their hidden grain, at last exposed in the 'for all time one sacrifice for sins' (Hebrews 10:12). Another illustration is that of a perennial plant: the flower of its first year is a true expression of the life of the plant, but, maybe, not till the fourth or fifth year will the full glory of that flower, the full 'meaning' of the plant, become apparent. So Jesus and Calvary are the full flowering which was always inherent in the perennial sacrifices (Hebrews 10:1–18).

(c) The death penalty is a matter on which Bible-loving interpreters differ. Did Jesus imply in John 8:1–11 that he was setting it aside? Some say 'yes' while others are equally sure that the state still has the right, after due process of law, to impose capital punishment.

To sort out such questions, and even to reach different conclusions, and then to live with each other within the authority of the Word of God, is (if it may be put like this) the 'fun' of having a Bible, but, whatever conclusion is reached, we must go on to ask why, and for what purpose, the Old Testament legislated as it did. The fundamental principle of Old Testament jurisprudence is the *lex talionis*, 'an eye for an eye' (Exodus 21:23–25; Leviticus 24:19–20; Deuteronomy 19:21). It is important to notice that these three references make the *lex talionis* a principle governing judicial sentencing. It is not a directive for personal action. (In Matthew 5:38–42 the Lord Jesus was rescuing the great regulation from this pharisaic misapplication, not crossing it out of the Bible!)

First, 'an eye for an eye' is not an expression of *savagery*; it is an insistence on *equity*. The sentence must match the offence – no more, no less. This rule was meant to guard against overreaction, excessive punishment, making some unfortunate 'an example'. It also guards against the leniency which takes an unduly relaxed attitude to some crimes or criminals. It calls for preciseness, impartiality, exactitude. Secondly, the Old Testament promises (Deuteronomy 19:20) that this exactness of retribution will act as a deterrent, and purge society. Thirdly, we presume that when the Old Testament calls for the death penalty, not only for violation of the sixth commandment but for all offences within the Decalogue, it was because no other legal imposition made the sentence fit the offence, or accorded the offender the dignity of being treated as a responsible human being, or (the central purpose of the

Old Testament) upheld the honour and sanctity of the law. If therefore the capital penalty is abandoned, the principle behind it must be safeguarded: the exact matching of punishment, crime and criminal, and demonstrating the dignity and sanctity of the law.

(d) Can we say that the Ten Commandments must surely still apply to Christians? Yes, but with due care. Today's older generations will recall that we were brought up under a pharisaic rather than a biblical understanding of the Fourth Commandment, and Sundays were often burdensome and illogical days. It was as if all the Bible ever said was 'no work on Sundays', and this was taken to mean 'no play either'. And with so many consequent absurdities! Very often the people who were foremost to impose 'sabbatarianism' were also the first to complain if the church caretaker had not been hard at it from an early Sabbath hour stoking the central heating. Tradition and thoughtlessness seemed to rule – and it wasn't OK. But the New Testament never quotes the Fourth Commandment, and verses like Colossians 2:16 should alert us to the need for thoughtfulness. How could a no-work-on-Sunday ethic be enforced in a slave-society? But Exodus 20:8 calls for 'remembrance' and Deuteronomy 5:12 for (literally) 'keeping', Exodus 23:12 legislates for a day of 'refreshment', and Isaiah 58 indicates that a properly kept Sabbath can be a very busy day indeed. In other words, we are called to obey, but taking the whole of Scripture into account, not just single verses, and possibly above all, to keep traditional interpretations under constant review and correction.

(e) The Lord Jesus overruled the Old Testament's food restrictions (Mark 7:19). So, we are free to decide our domestic diet, what we order in a restaurant, and to enjoy the delights of a nice bowl of snake soup in Hong Kong. Yes indeed, if that is what grabs you. 'Everything God created is good, and nothing is to be rejected if it is received with thanksgiving, because it is sanctified by the word of God and prayer' (1 Timothy 4:4–5). But do the food laws then say nothing today? And what about the prohibition of mixed material in clothing (Deuteronomy 22:11)? Not to mention cooking a young goat in its mother's milk (Exodus 23:19)? Part of the problem is that we are not told why these regulations were imposed, and we must always be ready to admit that our guesses may be wrong. It is likely, for example, that the rule about goats and their mothers' milk had to do with then current magical superstitions: that the resulting brew was a magic potion promoting fertility. Maybe this is the principle behind many regulations that seem especially strange to us. Food and clothing laws, avoiding pagan superstitions, and the like were all part of insisting that the Lord's people preserved and practised a distinctive lifestyle. Their basic distinctiveness (Deuteronomy 4:1–8) was of course moral and spiritual: their life of obedience to the Word of God. But smaller indications mattered – the way they ate and dressed, the way they ran the farm. All these things contributed to a proper separation from unbelievers, and a wholesome demonstration of a distinctive loyalty to the Lord. These issues matter today as much as they ever did, and we should be zealous to find ways of expressing our distinctiveness, including dress, diet and the refusal of the superstitions of the world around us.

All of life

In the Old Testament, the law of the Lord reached into every nook and cranny of life. No doubt the 'commanders of thousands' (Deuteronomy 1:15) dealt with large social issues, but the commanders 'of tens' applied God's Word to domestic issues, and the second person singular of the Decalogue (Exodus 20:3–17) made each and every individual responsible to live the life of God in the context of the day. A review of the ethical teaching of Jesus and the apostles shows that the same is true today: we are called to be a distinct people, with norms, characteristics, and habits – styles we adopt and practices we refuse – by which 'in a crooked and depraved generation' we 'shine like stars', holding on to and holding out 'the word of life' (Philippians 2:15–16).

Have a go at interpreting Moses' law for today

Days 1–3
Read through Exodus 20:22 – 23:19 with the following outline. Either read about thirty verses a day or read the whole passage on each of three days.

1. Prologue: the one God, and the altar as the one place of worship (20:22–26).
2. Ordering the household: care of servants (22:1–11).
3. Capital charges: social (21:12–27).
4. Responsibility for property and family (21:28 – 22:15).
   ▶ Animals (21:28–36).
   ▶ Ownership (22:1–15).
   ▶ Family (22:16–17).
5. Capital charges: religious (22:18–20).
6. Ordering relationships in the light of former servanthood (22:21 – 23:9).
7. Epilogue: the one God and the religious ordering of life (23:10–19).

Day 4
In what ways does the building of an altar (Exodus 20:22–26) apply to us, and in what ways does it not? Cf. Genesis 12:6–7; 13:3; Hebrews 13:9–12.

Day 5
Read Exodus 22:21; 23:9; cf. Deuteronomy 10:19–22. In what ways should our past, from which we have been redeemed by Jesus, direct and affect our relationships?

Day 6
Exodus 21:12–27; 22:18–20. In what ways do these regulations provide pointers for today's courts?

Day 7
Exodus 22:16–17. Should/could there be penalties for fornication today? How and what?

What a hope!

The uniqueness of the Lord Jesus Christ can be studied along some clear lines. There is the attested fact of his bodily resurrection from the dead, for example, and the moral majesty of his perfect life. In addition, there is his unparalleled influence for good throughout world history, and, what now concerns us, the wealth of prediction which binds the Old Testament to the New and the New to the Old around his towering and magnetic Person.

Fulfilment in the Gospels is of two sorts. There is deliberate, or 'obedience'-fulfilment, as, for example, in John 19:28. We surely cannot be mistaken to think that on the cross Jesus searched his vast knowledge of the Bible to make sure he had left nothing undone of all that was written about him, not even the dehydration described in Psalm 22:15. It was, then, not because he was dehydrated (though, as the crucified, he would have been) but in order that the Scripture might be fulfilled, that he said, 'I thirst.' The same chapter in John (verses 23–24; cf. verses 34–37) illustrates circumstantial fulfilment: cases where the agents were unaware that they were obeying the Bible, but where the Word of God imposed its will on events. Thus, all unknowing, the soldiers cast lots for Jesus' clothes, pierced his side, and left his bones unbroken. In these ways, then, the Old Testament flowed forward like a full and irresistible stream to its intended destination in Christ Jesus our Lord.

Moses' expectations: victor and prophet

In a very low-key way, when the Satan-serpent seduced Adam and Ishshah (later Eve) into denigrating the character of the Lord God, doubting his word and breaking his law (Genesis 3:1–6), the announcement was made that the 'seed' of the woman would deal a death-blow to the serpent (verse 15). It would be contrary to the literary methods of Genesis to elaborate or explain, but, within the terms of the narrative, what can this mean but that a truly human child will bring to an end the serpent's usurpation, and all its consequent woes (Revelation 12:1–11; 20:2, 10)?

What 'seed' this will be, or when, is left unsaid. Consistently with the ever-present spirit of expectation throughout the Old Testament, any and every next child could be the promised Child (cf. Genesis 5:8–29; 17:18–19; Isaiah 7:14; Micah 5:3–5). The same is true about Moses' significant messianic forecast. At Mount Sinai, Moses occupied a unique position. He was the one and only mediator of the Word of God to Israel (Exodus 19:9). When, therefore, in Deuteronomy 18:15–16, he predicted 'a prophet like me', and specifically recalled his own ministry at Horeb (Sinai), he had in mind someone uniquely special. In the same passage (verses 14, 21–22), Moses spoke in general terms of the ministry of prophets in Israel. In other words, there will be prophets, but Israel must always be on the lookout for The Prophet, the prophet like Moses. Just as every next child could be the promised 'seed', so every next prophet could be the unique Prophet. Deuteronomy 34:10 indicates how this expectation lived on in Israel (cf. John 1:21).

David's expectations: the Royal Priest, the Priestly King

In 2 Samuel 7:1–17 David purposed to build a house for the Lord, but was forbidden to do so. Rather, the Lord would build a house for David, an enduring line of kings (verses 11b–16). At some point, as time passed, this hope became focused on the coming of a great Son of David, yet to be born. So here too hope is alive in the Old Testament. Every next child, every next prophet – and now every next king may be the longed-for ideal – in this case, David come back again (cf. Ezekiel 34:23–24).

Within that general royal expectation, however, David had a particular contribution to make: the coming of Melchizedek, the Priest King. Melchizedek, whose name means 'king of righteousness', entered the Bible story unexpectedly in Genesis 14:18–20a. He was king of Salem (Jerusalem) and priest of 'God Most High, Creator/Possessor of heaven and earth'. Abram acknowledged that his royalty and his priesthood were genuine by giving him a tithe of the spoils he had taken from the four kings of the east. In addition, he identified Melchizedek's 'God Most High' with the God he himself worshipped by speaking at once of 'Yahweh (who is) God Most High' (verses 20b–22). In summary, then, we find unexpectedly that in Jerusalem in the time of Abram there was a king who was also a true priest, worshipping Yahweh as 'God Most High'.

Psalm 110

Melchizedek is not named again in the Bible until Psalm 110:4, a psalm which Jesus vouched for as written by David, putting its authorship beyond doubt. In verse 1, then, David speaks of 'the LORD (Yahweh)' and of 'my Lord'. This is the point Jesus took up in Mark 12:35–37. The coming Davidic Messiah is a son of David (2 Samuel 7:7–12; Isaiah 9:7; Matthew 1:1; Luke 1:32), so how can David call him 'Lord'? It was not a trick question, but a serious attempt to make his opponents face the fact that the Old Testament predicted a Messiah who was both a son of David and more than David's son and also a priest in the line of Melchizedek. But what, we may ask, would prompt David to think in these terms?

Very interestingly, at the time of Joshua, centuries after Abraham, the king of Jerusalem was called Adoni-Zedek, 'lord/sovereign of righteousness' (Joshua 10:3). This name has the same formation and meaning as Melchi-zedek. This suggests that, even if not the same dynasty (though why not?), the same kingship continued in Jerusalem, a line of priest-kings like Melchizedek. When David became king in Jerusalem (2 Samuel 5:6–9), he too 'became' Melchizedek, the priest-king, and since Abram had recognized this royal priesthood as a genuine priesthood of Yahweh, there is no reason why David too should not have done so, taking the idea of royal priesthood into his own royal house. In addition, 2 Samuel 8:18 says (literally) that 'David's sons were priests' (cf. NIV margin, ESV), thus suggesting that there was in Jerusalem a distinct priesthood, resident in the royal house, alongside and different from the priesthood of Aaron. And as he meditated on this, it 'came' to David that this was a true forecast of the Messiah, 'a priest upon his throne' (cf. Zechariah 6:13). Hebrews 5:5–6; 7:1–17 correctly understands this as fulfilled in the sacrificial and priestly ministry of the Lord Jesus Christ.

The Psalms' expectations: the larger-than-life King

Scattered through the Psalms are verses referring to the expected King. Gathering them together, a very great figure emerges, along these lines:

▶ Though he meets worldwide opposition (2:1–3; 110:1), yet through the Lord (2:6, 8; 18:46–50; 21:1–13; 110:1–2), he is victorious (45:3–5; 89:22–23), and establishes world rule (2:8–12; 18:43–45; 45:17; 72:8–11; 89:25; 110:5–6), centred on Zion (2:6), and noted for morality (45:4, 6–7; 72:2–3, 7; 101:1–8).

▶ His rule is everlasting (21:4; 45:6, 72:5), peaceful (72:7), prosperous (72:16), undeviatingly loyal to the Lord (72:15).

▶ The king is pre-eminent among men (45:2, 7), friend of the poor, and enemy of the oppressor (72:2–4, 12–14).

▶ In his kingdom, the righteous flourish (72:7); he is remembered for ever (45:17), and his name is everlasting (72:17).

▶ People give him unending thanks (72:15), and the Lord bestows everlasting blessing (45:2).

▶ He is heir to David's covenant (89:28–37; 132:11–12), and to Melchizedek's priesthood (110:4).

▶ He belongs to the Lord (89:18), is devoted to him (21:2, 7; 63:1–8, 11), and is his son (2:7; 89:27).

▶ He is seated at the Lord's right hand (110:1), and is himself God (45:6).

We do not have the information to trace the steps by which the initial promise of an enduring house (2 Samuel 7:1–17) matured into this expectation of a larger-than-life, human and divine figure. But, as we shall now see in Isaiah, this is indeed the way the Old Testament came to foresee the Messiah.

Isaiah's expectations: King, Servant and Conqueror

Isaiah painted the largest and most comprehensive messianic canvas in the Old Testament. In 2 Samuel 7:1–17 the Lord promised David an everlasting line of kings, a 'royal house'. But if we are right, above, about David and Melchizedek, then David himself came to look forward to a single king who would be the Melchizedek Priest. Indeed, the grim failure of David to live up to the promise of his earlier years, and the miserable decline of his character, kingship and kingdom, would have been enough to make thoughtful minds (including his own) say, 'Surely there must be something/someone better than this.' At any rate, by the time of Isaiah (c. 700 BC), the prophet could confidently predict the great, individual, divine messianic King. This is the leading messianic topic in the first section (chapters 1 – 37) of the book of Isaiah (9:1–7; 11:1–16.

As recorded in Isaiah 38 – 39, the faithless behaviour of King Hezekiah alerted Isaiah to the coming Babylonian captivity. The fact that the captivity did not occur for another hundred years, and the return not for another almost two hundred years, is not a problem. Babylon was a contender for world domination in Isaiah's day, and he does not mention dates, only facts: captivity and return. Such a message, coming loss and coming restoration, would have been a meaningful and crucial ministry to Isaiah's contemporaries. But, of course, as soon as he foretold captivity, and with it the end of the effective monarchy of David in Jerusalem (39:5–7), he had to face the question, What now becomes of the great messianic promises? The answer he was given was that the Messiah is more than a King; he is also a Saviour and Sin-bearer. Consequently, Isaiah 38 – 55 centre on his forecast of the Servant of the Lord, a figure of world significance (42:1–4), divinely prepared to restore Israel and to be the world's salvation (49:1–6), the totally obedient individual, even when his odedience involved the most extreme suffering (50:4–9), and the divine–human substitutionary sacrifice for sin (52:13 – 53:12).

The third division of the book of Isaiah is chapters 56 – 66. Look at it this way: the great work of sin-bearing and salvation has been completed in 52:13 – 53:12, but 56:1 says that 'salvation is close at hand'. Yes, salvation has been accomplished, but, equally yes, there is more to come. This is the purpose of chapters 56 – 66, to teach the Lord's people how to live as they await the salvation he plans to bring, or, for us, how to live in the interim between the finished work of salvation on the one hand, and the consummation of salvation on the other, between Calvary and the second coming. Accordingly, the messianic figure in Isaiah's third picture is the Conqueror. He brings his people into the full possession of salvation, and deals in a final way with all his enemies. His work is salvation and vengeance. The key passages are: Isaiah 59:21; 61:1–3 (cf. Luke 4:16–21); Isaiah 61:10 – 62:7; 63:1–6.

Please read through Isaiah's threefold portrait of the

Messiah. It is a huge canvas, indeed – what is properly called a 'triptych', three painted panels, each with its own subject, but hinged together to show they are essentially one. Isaiah emphasizes four truths in particular about the Messiah:

1. Individual

Isaiah looked forward to a single, individual Person who would be King, Servant/Saviour and Conqueror. The King is foreseen as the son of a virgin mother (7:14), a child who will be born (9:6) (is there anything more individual than birth?), a 'shoot' in the family tree of Jesse (11:1). The Servant is the Spirit-endowed individual (42:1), the single polished arrow in the Lord's quiver (49:2), the individual sufferer of 50:6, whose buoyant faith (50:7) contrasts so vividly with the despondency of the people (49:14), and the sin-bearing (53:6, 11), dead and buried (53:8–9), living and victorious (53:12) Arm of the Lord (53:1). The Conqueror is the Spirit-anointed preacher (61:1), rejoicing in the Lord (61:10), dressed in the garments of salvation as individually as a bridegroom or bride in wedding finery (61:10), and the solitary, majestic figure returning victorious from the fight (63:1).

Isaiah did not foresee some 'personification' of what he conceived the people of God ought to be. He was expecting an individual Man, and, as we know by hindsight, he was prefiguring Jesus 700 years before Bethlehem.

2. Universal

The Messiah would be the King, Saviour and Conqueror of the world. The immediate promise to David was of an enduring royal house (2 Samuel 7:16), but it would seem that, rapidly, a universal dimension was added. David himself saw the Melchizedek Priest-King as the conqueror of the nations (Psalm 110:5–6), a truth which actually arose from Genesis 14. The four great kings from the east had re-established their dominion over the west of the known world, but then they themselves were conquered and despoiled by Abram with his private army. In principle, then, Abram became the world's king, but at once he paid homage to Melchizedek, the lesser acknowledging the greater. Psalm 2 pictured world history as a conflict between the Lord's king and the kings of the earth, and called them to submit to him. Psalm 89 prays for the fulfilment of the Lord's double promise to David: universal, and unending rule (verses 20–25, 26–29). This is the king Isaiah predicted (Isaiah 9:7; 11:10, 14–16). Likewise, the Servant of the Lord comes on the scene with a Gentile mission (42:1–4). He is prepared by the Lord to be the world's salvation (49:6), and when he has finished his sin-bearing work (52:13 – 53:12), the call goes out to all who thirst to come to his banquet (55:1–13; cf. 25:6–10a). As for the Conqueror, it is true that his victory crushes the world which has opposed him (63:6), but it is also true that the glory he brings to Zion will be shared worldwide (62:1–2), for both the King (11:6–9) and the Conqueror (65:25) usher in the new creation, the new heaven and new earth of 65:17–20. It is on David's throne – that is, from Zion – that the king rules (9:7; cf. 33:17–24), but in 65:17–25 'Jerusalem' seems to be another name for the new heaven and new earth, not a specific geographical centre but a way of thinking about the new creation, the whole cosmos as a community organized by the Lord for his glory and his people's joy. This, of course, runs straight into New Testament thinking, in which those who believe in Jesus are already children of the heavenly Jerusalem (Galatians 4:26–31; Hebrews 12:22–24), enjoying a present citizenship (Philippians 3:20), and looking forward to the coming heavenly city (Revelation 21).

3. The divine–human Messiah

As Isaiah looked forward, he realized that no 'mere' descendant of David could be the King, Saviour and Conqueror that Israel and the world needed, and, as in other places in the Old Testament (e.g. Psalm 45:6; Malachi 3:1), he foresaw the coming of the Lord himself. The coming King is the 'mighty God' (Isaiah 9:6), a title given to Yahweh in 10:21. Indeed, it seems almost a matter of indifference to the prophet whether he speaks of the messianic King on his throne or the Lord on his throne (e.g. 24:21–23). The Servant is called 'the Arm of the Lord' in 53:1, a title given to the Lord in 51:9, picturing his saving activity at the Exodus (cf. Deuteronomy 26:8). In Isaiah 52:10, when it says, 'the Lord will lay bare his holy arm', the picture is of a person 'rolling up his sleeves' for action. The Servant is that Arm, the Lord himself stripped for action, come to save. The Conqueror does not seem to be explicitly stated to be divine. The emphasis throughout is on his enduement with the Lord's Spirit and Word (59:21; 61:1), his personal delight in the Lord (61:10), and his wholehearted commitment to the task he has been given (62:1). Nevertheless, 59:15b–18 describes the Lord himself donning the garments of salvation, because there is no-one else to do the work, but in 61:10 the same garments are given to the Conqueror. He is uniquely identified with the Lord, to say the least, and in 63:1 claims to be the one who is 'mighty to save' – that is, the Lord as described in 59:15b–17.

4. The return of David

This idea is not unique to Isaiah (cf. Ezekiel 34:23), but Isaiah does in fact unify his threefold picture of the Messiah around David. The King sits on David's throne (Isaiah 9:7), shoots from Jesse's root (11:1), but is also the root from which Jesse himself sprang (11:10). The portrayal of the Servant concludes with a 'tailpiece' (chapters 54 – 55) in which the Servant is identified with David (55:3–4). The Conqueror does what only David ever did: he conquers Edom (63:1), which in the Old Testament became a code word for the world in its ceaseless hostility to the Lord and his people (cf. Isaiah 34; Ezekiel 35; Amos 9:11–12).

Daniel's expectations: kingdoms in collision

The second half of the book of Daniel consists of a type of writing called 'apocalyptic'. The book of Revelation in the New Testament is the supreme example. 'Apocalyptic' deals heavily with symbols, patterns and pictures: kings and kingdoms are depicted as beasts; numbers and periods of time are used as codes, and so on. Apocalyptic has been a happy hunting ground by writers who want to use the Bible to draw up a calendar of events, past and future, finding facts, peoples, kings and kingdoms hidden within its symbolisms. No study of the Bible is devoid of profit, but the main intention of apocalyptic is rather to provide us with a perspective on history, and to assure us of the outcome. It sees all history as a clash of kingdoms: on the one hand, the kingdom of God, which will ultimately triumph, and on the other, the kingdoms of the world, which, powerful as they are and terrible as they can be, are nevertheless doomed. The delighted cry in Revelation 11:15 can be taken as a motto of apocalyptic: 'The kingdom of the world has become the kingdom of our Lord and of his Christ, and he will reign for ever and ever.' In the same way Daniel 2:31–45 (so easy to read) accurately expresses the spirit and overarching theme of apocalyptic.

The book of Daniel consists of some of the most marvellous stories in the Old Testament (chapters 1 – 6), followed by some of its most intricate symbolic writing. The two parts are related both broadly and specifically. In the historical section, the Judean Daniel faces (and outfaces) earth's super-rulers – men like Nebuchadnezzar (chapters 1 – 4), Belshazzar (chapter 5) and Darius (chapter 6). In other words, in the actual warp and woof of history, and in individual lives (including ours), there is a collision of kingdoms, and Daniel embodies the way the kingdom of God triumphs, for example, over the lifestyle (chapter 1), wisdom (chapter 2), ideology (chapter 3) and power (chapters 4 – 5), and ruthless determination – or silliness (chapter 6)? – of the world's empires and emperors. All this provides a 'platform of realism' from which to view the symbolic presentation of history in chapters 7 – 12. The symbols could easily appear unreal if we did not see them through the spectrum of the triumph of the kingdom of God over earthly kingdom-power, as exemplified in Daniel and his friends.

Daniel's expectations were therefore of the coming of a totally triumphant and unending spiritual kingdom and its King – 'one like a son of man, coming with the clouds of heaven' (Daniel 7:11–14; cf. Matthew 24:30; Mark 13:26; Luke 21:27). His book is a cleverly integrated whole. Just as the history section as a whole prepares for the apocalyptic section, so individual stories throw light on individual apocalyptic visions. The four kingdoms of Daniel 2:1–49 prepare for the four kingdoms of 7:1–28, with the kingdom which crushes all kingdoms (2:44–45) finally realized in the princely Son of Man and the saints of the Most High (7:13–14, 27). Chapters 3 and 8 focus more on a clash of ideologies. In 3:1–30 Nebuchadnezzar tries to impose a world theology and worship, as though it were his right to determine the nature of God and religion. In 8:1–27, we learn that this ideological imperialism will continue right to the end, climaxing in an actual king rising up against the 'Prince of princes' (8:25), only to be destroyed. Daniel 4 records the smiting and healing of Nebuchadnezzar, but in 9:26 it is, surprisingly, the Anointed One himself who is 'cut off'. By this death (9:24, literally) 'rebellion' is finished, 'sins' are sealed away, the atonement price is paid for 'iniquity', everlasting righteousness is brought in, and the Holy of Holies is anointed. This glorious list, seen in the light of Scripture, describes how Adam's 'rebellion' is concluded in Christ, 'sin' is finally dealt with, now sealed away to trouble no more, atonement for 'iniquity' is made by paying the covering price, Christ's everlasting righteousness is provided to clothe his elect, and the Holy of Holies, the indwelling of the Lord in his people (Exodus 29:42–46; Leviticus 16:15–16) reaches its intended fulfilment (John 2:19–21; Ephesians 2:19–22; Revelation 21:3, 22–27). The final parallel in Daniel (5:1–30; 10:1 – 12:3) concerns the flow of history and the Lord's final victory. Daniel 5 is bracketed by, on the one hand, the record of the hubris of Belshazzar in assuming that the Lord's precious articles of worship could with impunity be used as the playthings of his dissolute court (verses 1–4), and, on the other, his downfall and death (verse 30) at the hands of 'Darius the Mede'. The final reality which this prefigures in miniature is the huge upheaval of the End, the suffering it brings to the Lord's people, and the final victory of 'Michael, the great prince' (12:1–3).

Such a brief review does scant justice to the brilliance of the history writing of chapters 1 – 6 and the compellingly intricate symbols of chapters 7 – 12, but it does highlight the central point: the collision of kingdoms, the world-wide canvas of the portrayal, the spiritual conflict at the heart of history, and the unfolding mystery of evil until, dramatically and finally, the kingdom of God prevails. Above all else, the book of Daniel demonstrates that 'the Most High is sovereign over the kingdoms of men' and 'Heaven rules' (4:25–26).

And much, much more

Immense as these expectations are, they do not exhaust the forward and upward gaze of the Old Testament.

▶ Jeremiah looked forward to the new covenant, resting on a full and final dealing with sin (31:31–34).

▶ Ezekiel saw the coming glory as the fulfilment of what the tabernacle and temple essentially meant: the indwelling of the Lord in the midst of his people (Exodus 29:42–46). In 1 Kings 8:27, at the dedication of his temple, Solomon asked, 'But will God really dwell on earth?', to which, amazingly, the answer must be 'Yes', for this was the whole purpose of the 'house', the Lord's 'address' at the centre of his people's life. Ezekiel the priest (1:1) was understandably enamoured with this idea, and brought his book to its climax (chapters 40 – 48) with a sketch of this ideal, not even a ground plan for an actual temple to be built, but 'a vision of truth'. The Lord Jesus Christ is the 'house'. Where he is, there God dwells among his people (John 2:18–22); we, who believe in Jesus, are the house, individually (1 Corinthians 3:16) and collectively (6:19), in which God dwells by his Spirit (Ephesians 2:11–22). The full reality is yet to come (Revelation 21:1–4, 22–27; 22:1–5).

It is important to insist that to allow the earthly Jerusalem of the Old Testament to blend forward in this way into the heavenly Jerusalem of the New is not a sort of conjuring trick. Within the Old Testament itself, the 'world-Jerusalem' of Isaiah 65 and the 'strong city' of Isaiah 24 – 27 (cf. 25:6–10a; 26:1–3) are no longer geographical locations. No earthly city could be the gathering place for all the nations, the messianic banquet. The animal sacrifices blended forward into the one sacrifice for sins forever, the cross of Calvary, and did so, not by denying their truth or abandoning their God-given significance, but by finally becoming what they always were. Territorial promises reach their destination in the kingdom not of this world, and the geographical Jerusalem becomes, as it was always intended to be, the heavenly. Joel expressed the expectation that the Lord would yet share his Sprit with 'all flesh' (Joel 2:28–32, NKJV; cf. Isaiah 32:15; 44:1–5; Ezekiel 36:24–27; 37:14; Acts 2:14–21, 38; 5:32).

But the list is pretty endless. The Old Testament without the New is unfinished; the New without the Old is unexplained. The Bible is one whole, single, marvellous book.

A week with Isaiah and the vision of Calvary

Nothing illustrates more clearly the forward gaze of the Old Testament than the fact that one of the most profound meditations on the cross of Christ was written 700 years before his birth, in Isaiah 52:13 – 53:12.

Day 1
52:13–15. 'Wisely' (verse 13) equally means 'successfully'. This is a 'success story', embodying a threefold exaltation (13), unparalleled suffering (14) and universal cleansing.

Day 2
53:1–2. The Servant is very ordinary and unimpressive – truly human (2) – but also uniquely special, the Arm of the Lord, the Lord himself acting to save (verse 1; cf. 52:10).

Day 3
53:3–5. His evident suffering and sorrow (verse 3) resulted from his identification with us (4). People did not recognize him; indeed, they rejected and misunderstood him (3b, 4). Nevertheless, his sufferings were 'for' – that is, 'because of / arose out of' – our sins.

Day 4
53:6. Something about all of us; something about each of us; something about the Lord.

Day 5
53:7–9. He deserved none of it, yet accepted it all by self-submission and self-restraint, even to the point of death. Note that in verse 9, 'wicked' is plural, and 'rich' is singular: 'wicked men' … 'rich man' (cf. Matthew 27:38, 57).

Day 6
53:10. Our salvation is something the Lord willed, desired. He achieved it through his Servant's death (verse 10a), but the Servant is alive to see those he has saved and to promote the spread of salvation (10cd). The 'guilt-offering' covered every aspect of sin, towards people we have hurt as well as towards God, whom we have offended. This is full salvation.

Day 7
53:11–12. Try this for a translation: '(What arises) from the toil of his soul, he will see with satisfaction. By his knowledge the Righteous One, my Servant, will provide righteousness for the many: he will shoulder their iniquities himself. Therefore I will apportion the many to him, and the strong he will apportion as spoil, just because he poured out his soul to death, and he let himself be numbered with

rebels, and himself bore the sin of many, and interposed for the rebels.'

Question

How is your knowledge of the Lord Jesus Christ enhanced by these passages of Old Testament Scripture? As a group or an individual, turn this knowledge into adoration and praise.

Books for further reading

Bible background

D. & P. Alexander (eds.), *The Lion Handbook to the Bible* (Lion Publishing, 2002).

Michael Eaton, *Ecclesiastes* (Tyndale Old Testament Commentary, 1983), p. 41.

Alec Motyer, *A Scenic Route through the Old Testament* (IVP, 1994); *Look to the Rock, The Old Testament and our Understanding of Christ* (IVP, 1996); *The Story of the Old Testament: Men with a Message* (Angus Hudson, 2001)

Stephen Motyer, *The Bible with Pleasure* (Crossway Books, 1997).

J. W. Wenham, *Christ and the Bible* (Tyndale Press 1972).

Bible commentaries

The best help when reading straight through a Bible book is *The New Bible Commentary: 21st Century Edition* (IVP, 1994). Its strength is making the flow of a book clear.

Always take advice before buying commentaries on individual Bible books.

Look out for these three IVP series:

The Crossway Bible Guides (eds., Ian Coffey and Stephen Gaukroger).

The Bible Speaks Today (eds., Alec Motyer and John Stott).

The Tyndale Bible Commentaries (eds., Donald Wiseman and Leon Morris).

Bible versions

If you have the opportunity to learn biblical Hebrew or New Testament Greek, seize it with both hands. These are the languages the Lord God chose to be the vehicles of revealed truth, therefore they are to be prized above any and all translations. Don't try to learn both Hebrew and

Greek together unless you have a linguistic gift and unlimited time at your disposal.

Without a working knowledge of Hebrew and Greek, there is safety in numbers. If you customarily use an older translation for your Bible reading, keep a more recent translation to hand, and vice versa. Allow different translations to throw light on each other. As a general rule, the older translations are more 'literal' (word specific), and the newer translations are in varying degrees 'dynamic equivalents', expressing biblical truth as it would be expressed today.

Here are some recommended Bible versions:

King James or Authorized Version (KJV / AV, 1611)
New King James Version or Revised Authorized Version (NKJV / RAV, 1982)
The Revised Version (RV, 1881, 1884), along with its reappearance as the New American Standard Bible (NASB, 1963)
English Standard Version (ESV, 2001)

There is an abundance of 'dynamic equivalent' versions. Their value is that they generally succeed in making the Bible text meaningful and plain. But it should be remembered that they do this in a way that runs miles beyond what the word-for-word versions would consider proper, by fixing on and clarifying whatever single interpretation appeals to the translator, and in this way they foreclose the options of meaning which the 'literal' translations leave open. We are much more in the hands of the translator, and the gap between translating and interpreting has greatly narrowed. The benefits and dangers of this are equally obvious. The two most widely used 'dynamic equivalent' translations are the Good News Bible (GNB, 1976) and the New International Version (NIV, most recent revision, 1984). The NIV is now available in a revised and gender-inclusive form as Today's New International Version (TNIV, 2005). There are also the Jerusalem Bible (JB, 1976), the New Living Translation (NLT, 1996), the New

English Bible (NEB, 1970) and, in its revised form, the Revised English Bible (REB, 1989).

Concordances

A good concordance is a great aid in understanding the Bible. Bible words have specific Bible meanings, and a concordance enables us to chase up a word in an English version, first, to its Hebrew or Greek parent, and then to find all the places in the Bible where that word is used, however it may have been translated into English. In this way we discover its 'ambience' or range of meaning by the way it is used.

The two best concordances (based on the Authorized / King James Version) are *Young's Analytical Concordance* (Lutterworth, 1939) and *Strong's Exhaustive Concordance* (MacDonald Publishing Co., 1993). A concordance to the NIV is also available.